RAPID VIDEO DEVELOPMENT FOR TRAINERS

How to Create Learning Videos Fast and Affordably

JONATHAN HALLS

Alexandria, Virginia

15 14 13 12   1 2 3 4 5 6 7 8 9 10

ASTD Press is an internationally renowned source of insightful and practical information on workplace learning and performance topics, including training basics, evaluation and return on investment, instructional systems development, e-learning, leadership, and career development. Visit us at www.astd.org/astdpress.

Ordering information: Books published by ASTD Press can be purchased by visiting ASTD's website at store.astd.org or by calling 800.628.2783 or 703.683.8100.

Library of Congress Control Number: 2012935932
ISBN-10: 1-56286-811-X
ISBN-13: 978-1-56286-811-6

ASTD Press Editorial Staff:
Director: Anthony Allen
Senior Manager, Production & Editorial: Glenn Saltzman
Community of Practice Manager, Learning Technologies: Justin Brusino
Associate Editor: Heidi Smith
Editorial and Production: Abella Publishing Services, LLC
Cover Design: Mazin Abdelgader and Lon Levy

Printed by Versa Press, Inc., East Peoria, IL, www.versapress.com

Rapid Video Development

Table of Contents

Chapter 2 VIDEO PSYCHOLOGY

Chapter 3 VIDEO AND LEARNING

Chapter 7 THE SPOKEN WORD LAYER

Chapter 8 THE MUSIC AND SOUND EFFECTS LAYER

Section 3: Preproduction

Chapter 9 PREPRODUCTION WORKFLOW

Section 4: Production

Chapter 10 TOOLS OF VIDEO PRODUCTION

Chapter 11 HOW TO SHOOT GREAT PICTURES

Chapter 12 HOW TO USE YOUR CAMERA

Chapter 13 LOOKING GOOD IN VIDEO

Section 5: Postproduction

Chapter 14 EDITING YOUR VIDEO

Section 6: Into Action

Chapter 15 TECH STUFF

Preface

Workplace learning professionals, or trainers as most people know us, hold a key role of leading people to the future in today's organizations. And because of our important role in tomorrow's organizations, we are charged with educating, inspiring, motivating, and correcting performance.

Because of this, we are constantly updating our professional tool kit with new skills to expand our learning influence in organizations, while at the same time keeping costs down. Multimedia communication is a new skill for trainers in the 21st century—one we need to add to existing professional competencies such as facilitation, instructional design, influencing the C-suite, and writing workbooks. Of all the multimedia skills, video is probably the most complex.

Technology has catapulted us into a new era where video is no longer the exclusive domain of TV and film producers. You don't need expensive production crews to make video anymore, nor do you need expensive cameras. But you do need an understanding of how video works as a communication method, skills to produce it, and the discipline to do it well. Without these, you leave the success of your video to chance. It may end up looking amateur and achieve the same level of impact as a poorly designed training class delivered by someone not skilled in facilitation.

Don't Leave Your Video to Chance

I've written this book so you don't have to leave your video to chance. I want to help you develop the disciplines of planning video content to facilitate learning and to do it professionally. We will look at what you can do to make the flow of your content smooth and professional, as well as how to shoot in a way that prevents your video from looking amateurish. We'll examine what makes a powerful video and then review it through the lens of how people learn. It's these sets of disciplines that will ensure your video content becomes a key part of your tool kit to help drive organizational performance through learning.

I've been teaching media in newspapers, radio, and television organizations for more than 20 years. However, I have spent an increasing amount of time over the past three years working with government and corporate organizations that want to take advantage of accessible technology and create media in learning. Increasingly, nonmedia organizations see media production and communication as a key skill set their staffs need. I've seen this firsthand. Three years ago, organizations would send one or two people to my workshops. Today, these organizations ask me to teach their entire training departments. Media production skills are hot.

Workshop Structure

Based on my work as both a teacher and a practitioner, I have structured this book in much the same way that I structure my workshops. I feel this is the most productive way to help you. Fortunately, my publishers have been kind enough to let me write in a more personal style rather than make this a rigid old textbook. I like to see learning as a conversation, and so I have written conversationally.

In this book, I explain how video works as a method of communication by deconstructing it into a series of message layers. I find this is the fastest and most effective way to learn the power of video. This may not be how some film schools teach the psychology of video, but that's fine, because we're looking at producing web video—not films. And while this is also not a book on television production, there will be some similarities between filmmaking, television, and web video in the concepts we discuss, such as visual grammar and editing.

This is a book on web video and how to create web video for learners—not how to make cinema or television video. If it were a book on television or film, I would have approached it differently, because each medium has a different physical relationship with the viewer, and as a consequence requires a different approach. (And actually, web video is not a medium like TV and cinema. It is a method of communication that sits on the medium of the web.)

There are a few other things about this book I'd like to share. First, you'll find that certain techniques and the language of describing things are different than what you may have heard before depending on which country you work in, or whether you are in television or cinema. For example, some people use the term *long shot* while other people say *mid-shot*. Both words have the same meaning. And some people use the term *crab left* to describe what others call *truck left*. Does it matter which term you use? I don't think so, as long as you are consistent. And to be consistent, I have adopted some terms over others. At the end of the day, the goal is to make video that aids learning.

Finally, I have often seen the skills and time required to create quality video play second fiddle to things like choosing learning management systems (LMS) and other more macro-level issues. Neither the LMS nor the content is more important than the other. An LMS has little value if you don't also invest in the quality of your video. I'm not suggesting a conspiracy here. This just happens for one reason or another—perhaps building technology is easier to quantify. I am hoping this book helps restore the balance so organizations invest the necessary time and money, because well-produced video, and indeed well-produced content of any type, is what breathes life into learning technology.

Good Luck

Although making video is much harder than it looks and takes longer to produce than most people think, it is loads of fun and hugely rewarding in terms of its effect on learning, along with the time and money it saves an organization. As you develop your skills and discipline in making video, I hope you find that the access we now have to affordable video technology improves your practice as a trainer, so you can deliver greater value to your organization and demonstrate the value of learning to all you influence.

Acknowledgments

It's easy to be proud when you write a book. But its success really sings the praises of the people who have contributed to it and shaped your thinking over the years. ASTD Press has a great team. Thanks to Justin Brusino for asking me to write this and badgering me to write for some years now. Heidi Smith, my editor, smoothed out my prose, giving it more life and translating some of the cultural terms I have picked up from around the world into American English. Anthony Allen, ASTD's director of production, was my second set of technical eyes on production and technical issues. And Amanda Anderson shot the video for the interactive e-book.

Thanks also to the thought leaders I interviewed and included in the book. What I teach is as much the result of people who have shaped my development as it is my own critical reflection. The late Alex Vale inspired in me the spirit of media and learning. Bruce McNeilly coached me and shaped my early professional years. At the BBC, Paul Myers and Phil Ross taught me new media when it was still new, as did Simon Fox, who also taught me television production. Simon was part of BBC Production Training's Elstree team, which gave me the best television education anyone could want, along with the privilege of serving the team as its boss. These guys are the best media trainers in the world, and the time I worked with them was the proudest period in my career. Mhairi Campbell and Gordon Lamont, two former BBC education editors, have also been influential as both friends and colleagues.

Thanks to my family. My parents always encouraged me, and my wife Sharon is a constant support. Not only does she endure my constant critiques of everything I see on television, read in the newspaper, and hear on the radio, but also, she listens to my ideas, encourages me, and acts as the first, second, and third set of eyes whenever I write.

In This Book and on the Web

Throughout this book, still photographs are shown to illustrate concepts discussed in the text. All are taken by Jonathan Halls, except where noted. The photos are a good visual representation of the ideas and skills needed in video production. For fine-tuning of the techniques, please go to www.astd.org/rapidvideo. There you will find videos titled by technique, for easy access to each skill you want to see in more detail. Since this book is about video, video is the best medium to show these techniques in action.

(photo by Shutterstock)

Section 1:

Behind the Video

There is an important need for multimedia literacy. This means understanding the methods of communication that include audio, video, online text, animation, gaming, and database generation. This book focuses on one of these methods: video. It's fair to say that not all video is created equal. You have video that is shot for cinema, video that is shot for television, and video that is shot for the web. Each is different and is experienced differently. The focus of this book is making video for viewing on the web. While you'll find many similarities with television production, this is not a TV production handbook.

We will look at what is necessary for what's known as single-camera shooting. This book is all about affordable single-camera video work. If you work in a television studio, you will work with multiple cameras, and this is known as multi-camera production. That is not covered in this book, either.

This first section is about the thinking and processes you will use in your single-camera web video. It deals with video and the trainer, video psychology, video and learning, and video in practice.

CHAPTER ONE

Video and the Trainer

In this chapter:

- The evolution of video in the training room and the opportunities web video offers workplace learning professionals
- How video has become easier for trainers to produce custom-fit video for their learning projects and has become more accessible for learners
- Where workplace learning professionals can use didactic video
- The emergence of multimedia skills as a 21st century skill set for trainers

---

It's Not New

Video in the training room is not new. In fact, workplace learning professionals have been using video in training sessions for many years. What is new is the opportunity to make professional-looking video ourselves, as well as the accessibility to that video. And while the opportunity to produce fast, targeted video that facilitates learning is exciting, working with video has not always been easy.

Yesterday

Showing video in a training class 20 years ago often involved a leap of faith. You had to roll a heavy television set and clunky old VHS player into the seminar room and hope all the wires were plugged into the right sockets. Switching everything on in front of a room of learners was often stressful. The trainer who used the equipment the day before may have broken it and forgotten to report it. Or she may have fiddled with some of the settings, so the video would look snowy or would have a blue tinge.

In the past, video was often a necessary evil rather than an opportunity.

Today

The good news is that today, VHS tapes are mostly a thing of the past and technology is smarter. We now use DVDs or video files saved on our laptops for classroom training. If we have access to the Internet, we may stream the videos directly from video sites such as YouTube or Vimeo. And if we don't use a data projector, we plug our laptops or DVD players into large flat-screen monitors that automatically detect and adjust all those troublesome settings.

Advances in technology mean that using video for learning no longer requires learners to flock to a classroom and sit in impatience as the trainer struggles with the remote control. We can now take video to the learner.

It's all really exciting. Never before has video offered so many opportunities to create learning solutions that are so tailored and flexible. Blending online video with interactive online conversations, social media learning, and in-class face-to-face learning means that we can now shape the learning experience with precision to make it even more learner-centered. Because not only can you give the remote control to each and every learner, but you can also let them watch when they want at a pace that best suits their learning speed. They can also watch from wherever they are with whatever they want: on their PC at the office or workshop floor; on their laptop sitting in an airport terminal; with their phone as they look up critical 'how-tos'; as they do their work; or on their tablet as they sit in the park.

The way we deliver video is not the only thing that has changed.

Now You Can Make It

Twenty years ago, if you wanted a management training video, you had to find a catalog, then either buy it or borrow it from a library. And buying video was never cheap. If you worked for a large enough company, you may have been given some budget to commission a video, but commissioning a video was never cheap either. Never easy. Never quick. And you could not be sure your production team fully understood or cared about your message and its need to facilitate learning.

Today, technology has changed so much that you can create the video yourself for next to no cost, quickly and easily. You don't need to struggle with the creative director of a video production house who wants to achieve a look and feel for your video that suits his artistic temperament rather than meets your learning objective.

You can do it all yourself. And that is what the massive changes in media over the past decade have brought us: more power, control, and flexibility.

The Key Changes: Technology and Distribution

Technology has advanced to:

- reduce cost of production and improve technical quality
- make production easier through superior technical options
- dramatically cut costs in video distribution.

Cheaper and Better

Advancements in technology have made video production equipment cheaper than ever before. You can buy a camera at domestic electronics stores like Best Buy or Fry's that shoots video in high definition for less than $300. And the quality of these cameras—while not broadcast quality—is exceptional and ideal for online video. Manufacturers achieve this quality with plastic lenses and electronic gadgetry that we couldn't even dream of 10 years ago.

In the broadcasting world, cameras continue to be cheaper too. To buy a broadcast-quality camera 10 years ago, you had to shell out $10,000 to $20,000, and this would often not include the lens. Today, television networks are shooting on HDV cameras that cost less than $5,000.

The other piece of equipment that has become cheaper has been the editing suite. Or should we call it a suite at all? Traditional video production took place in a room known as the editing suite. In this room, a visual editor would compile the final video using several video players. Go back 15 years and an editing suite would cost you $75,000 or more to both buy and wire together.

Video editing suites were a fixture of television production. News crews would shoot on location, and then rush back to the station to hand their tapes over to a video editor, who spent his days in a dimly lit room with several television monitors, combining the raw footage into the finished product you saw on television.

Today, you can do everything the editor did on his expensive equipment plus more, using a piece of editing software that costs virtually nothing. Some of this software costs less than a hundred dollars and will deliver broadcast-quality results. And if you're running the software on a laptop, you can edit your video anywhere you like—immediately after you've shot your video on location, if you want.

So equipment has become cheaper. It has also become better.

Easier to Use

The other significant change in technology has been how manufacturers make video equipment easier to use.

Professionals don't like auto settings on cameras. One of the reasons is that traditionally, auto settings have never been as effective as manual settings at achieving precisely the picture you want. However, the auto settings on both consumer and prosumer cameras have improved incredibly. Prosumer cameras are a hybrid that sits between the consumer and the professional levels. They tend to have more manual functionality than consumer cameras, which are loaded with auto settings. But they still lack some of the manual controls expected on professional cameras. These improvements to entry-level cameras have made consumer and prosumer cameras easier for nonprofessionals to operate and capture good-looking video. Having fewer buttons to press and fewer settings to stress over makes it easier to aim and shoot your video.

Plus, the new cameras include all sorts of features designed to make your shots look better. The ease of use beats the complexity of the professional cameras of 10 years ago that had myriad buttons and settings. So technological advancements have made video cheaper and easier to make. And they've enabled the quality to skyrocket above levels we saw in stodgy VHS cameras.

Cheaper to Distribute

The Internet has revolutionized video distribution. If you were making industrial video, you'd shoot and edit it on equipment that cost a lot of money. You'd then duplicate it onto VHS tapes (or some other form of yesterday technology like laser discs), and then print stickers and covers, package it, and send it to customers in the mail.

If you didn't duplicate the tapes yourself, you'd create a master tape and send it to someone who did. With any luck, they'd do the mailing for you, although often, they'd be sent back for you to ship to your customers. Before the Internet, we didn't blink an eye over this process.

But now, instead of making master copies and sending them through a cumbersome duplication process, we simply upload the video files to a video server, using the Internet. Customers download and watch your video in their own time, wherever they happen to be. Cool, huh?

The way the Internet has revolutionized distribution is amazing. And you can create your own video and become a distributor or broadcaster using YouTube, Vimeo, or your own streaming server. No more postage.

For television broadcasters, this is very significant. TV stations maintain expensive transmitters and antenna towers. These require electricity for the transmitter and the blinking red light that sits at the top of the tower to prevent aircraft from flying into it.

Transmission costs money for the land the tower sits on, as well as for ongoing expenses like a fresh paint job every year to stop corrosion from bird droppings. TV stations with these massive overheads now compete with video publishers who have no transmission costs at all.

Technology has slashed the cost of distribution. And unlike TV transmission that has a limited range, the Internet has made the new free distribution international.

Internet Distribution Quality

While using the Internet radically changes distribution and opens up possibilities, it has a significant downside: quality. The video quality on the Internet is generally not as good as what you see on a DVD. It's certainly not as good as what you see on Blu-ray. The reason for this is limited bandwidth. (We discuss bandwidth further in chapter 15.)

We could discuss many other changes that have been made, but these are the main ones that affect learning. Understanding these changes and how they affect your ability to produce and distribute learning video is incomplete without also looking at what doesn't change.

What Does Not Change

Some things will likely never change, such as the reasons that people use video. Think of the media world in which newspapers are struggling for survival today. The smart newspapers have transformed their operations from paper and ink to multimedia.

They're still telling stories, but are doing it by including audio and video online with their text-based stories. The human need for stories will never change because that's how our brains are wired. The media companies that crashed forgot what doesn't change—the story. They built their businesses around technologies and fads, not around storytelling. We need to remember that with web video.

When it comes to videos about learning, we need to remember that video is merely another tool to help us do what we're hired to do: that is, deliver learning that helps people and organizations change. We don't do video because it's the new thing. Or because making video sounds like a lot fun (which of course it is).

There are other things that fall into the "not everything has changed" category: First, creating good video requires discipline. Like any communication, having good technology like an easy-to-operate camera does not make your message better or worse. You still need to learn the discipline of creating a visual message, understand how the medium works to convey that message powerfully, and make sure your message is anchored to your learning objectives. And you still need much planning to make sure it's successful.

Second, developing video skills takes time and effort. You don't become a video whiz overnight. It takes time to learn how to structure a video message and develop its narrative, as it does to use the camera correctly and get shots that are well-lit, are clearly focused, can easily convey the message, and are cut together well.

Third, creating learning videos requires an approach steeped in good learning practice. Sure, video needs to be interesting and contain elements of entertainment. But we're looking at learning video as an educational tool. So we need to draw together the psychology of video with the psychology of learning, which we do in chapters 2 and 3.

Video for Learning

Video offers endless possibilities to workplace learning professionals and organizations that want to improve communication and reinforce learning. Web video is ideal for:

- Classroom learning—use in a classroom.
- E-learning—use as part of online modules that staff can take anywhere they have a connection to your network at any time they like.
- Social media learning—use as a delivery method and also as a way of developing user-generated self-learning to share and improve knowledge management.
- Mobile learning—use in the field for just-in-time learning on a mobile phone or tablet.

Video can: save costs by eliminating the need to travel to a face-to-face class; make it easier for people in demanding jobs who find it difficult to leave their workplace for more than a few hours to access training; and remove that post-9/11 travel stress for people who need to catch a flight in order to gain professional development.

Using Video for Learning

Video doesn't just allow us to bring learning closer to the learner. It also enables us to:

- offer better demonstrations
- manipulate pictures to enrich learning
- offer regular access to experts
- maintain consistent standards in information delivery.

Let's consider these in more detail.

Better Demonstrations

Imagine you're attending a cooking class. For argument's sake, say you arrive late and find the only available seats are in the back of the room. In a cooking class that requires you to observe how a sauce caramelizes or changes form, you need to be up close—sometimes closer than the teacher.

A video camera can capture more up-close detail than a person who struggles to see over another student's shoulders, showing the actual caramelization process in more detail than a mere cooking demonstration.

Manipulate Pictures to Enrich the Learning

Video is not just about getting closer to the action than you would in a classroom; it also enables you to play with time. If you demonstrate a complex psychomotor skill in a classroom, you have to do it in real time. Shoot it on video, and you can break down the task into key steps, repeat those steps, show key steps in slow motion, and then repeat the whole process in real time. Talk about an unbeatable learning demonstration experience. These are all things you can't do in real life, but can in an editing suite.

Offer Regular Access to Experts

Another benefit of video is that you can add credibility by bringing an expert into your learning situation. You can't have the chief scientist visiting every face-to-face training session to explain a new pharmaceutical; he'd have no time to do his day job. However, you can shoot a video of him explaining the new drug, and then show it to all your classes or include it in your e-learning program. And, if your subject matter expert is a boring presenter, you can edit the video in a way that gives her presentation a little more life.

Maintain Consistent Standards in Information Delivery

Another benefit of learning video is that you develop more standardization; if different trainers teach the same skill at different times and in different locations, they may do it differently. A video demo ensures that your learners get the same demo every time.

21st Century Trainer Skills

Today it is generally accepted that the average trainer will have, along with her industrial expertise, skills in instructional design processes and group facilitation. That is, she can both design and deliver face-to-face training. In recent years, additional skill sets have been added to what many trainers are expected to have in their training tool kits: business acumen, organizational knowledge, and increasingly, virtual facilitation skills for events such as webinars.

However, these skills will not be enough in the future. Trainers will also need to be proficient in multimedia content creation and production, because multimedia communication will be a core skill of tomorrow's professional. Any person who needs to communicate in his job needs to be proficient at multimedia communication. But in the learning profession, there will come a time when multimedia production skills, such as video production, move from desired to essential criteria on job descriptions.

This scares some people, but it shouldn't. This fear often comes from the assumption that multimedia skills are largely technical. They're not. While multimedia has a technical component to it, it is less about gadgets than it is about content. We need technical skills to fire up Microsoft Word, but these skills are not what make a good piece of writing.

The multimedia trainer will be more an expert in multimedia content than in multimedia technology. And instead of knowing every piece of technology and software known to humanity, she will in fact have the skill of being able to learn it quickly when necessary.

Later in this book, we'll focus more on content than on gadgets and buttons. And when we talk about technology, it will be about what you need to know rather than what might happen to be the latest fad.

Developing the multimedia competencies of content development involves much about communication and learning. Communication and learning are closely related. I define communication as the process of creating shared understanding. And I see learning as taking communication one step further so that shared understanding is followed by retention and application.

The skills of making learning video are founded in the disciplines of media and learning. But as we discuss later in section 1, they work wonderfully together.

CHAPTER TWO

Video Psychology

In this chapter:

- Core principles for making engaging video content
- How the viewer's brain processes your video messages
- Web video's relationship to the viewer
- Stories and narrative
- New media attributes of web video

Elements of Video

When you kick back and watch television, it's easy to get lost in the story and miss all of the details that work to create powerful content. Television serials like *CSI* and *Burn Notice* are packed with visual and auditory data that work together to create a gripping narrative.

Just about everything you see in these television shows is in the picture for a reason. The way they move the camera, frame the shot, or add music affects your perception and understanding of their message. The objects you see in each shot—whether it is a carefully placed cell phone, pair of sunglasses, or bottle of soda—are there for a reason. Often the power comes not from an object that has been positioned in a shot, but from what has been left out.

The better a television producer or cinematographer understands the power and balance of all these objects, the more compelling their content. Masters like Alfred Hitchcock and Steven Spielberg spend time worrying about tiny distractions in each frame because they know they will transform the viewer's experience and profoundly affect their message.

Of course the converse is true too. Forgetting an object or putting too many objects in a shot could water down your message or distract the viewer from what you are trying to convey. Sometimes poorly planned pictures can undermine your message, while your camera work may distract so the audience tunes out. You may use too much music, too little, or the wrong style.

Video communication is complex and if you are serious about creating good video, you need to understand how it all works together. One way to understand video communication is to see it as a series of message layers. But before we consider the message layers, we need to understand some core principles about video communication. We're going to look at four core principles of video, video message layers, and how video works in the new media age.

Core Video Principles

Four core principles underpin the success of your video. They are:

- Video is lifeless without action.
- Pictures are the foundation of video.
- Video is not always the best way to communicate.
- Effective video is quick and easy to understand.

Let's consider each one in turn.

Principle 1: If There's No Action, Don't Use Video

Video is about watching things happen. If there is no movement or change in what people see, your viewers will quickly lose interest. This is why videos of a trainer giving a lecture almost always make it tougher on the learner.

Principle 2: Pictures Are the Foundation of Video

Every editorial decision you make in video must be made in reference to your pictures. When you plan your story, you should plan which pictures you will use before adding music, sound effects, and commentary.

Principle 3: Video Is Not Always the Best Communication Method

Because video is visual, certain types of information will not work well with video. For example, complex information with a lot of data never works well on video because it is not visual. This is why we tend to remember the satellite maps from TV weather reports rather than what the meteorologist said.

Many forms of learning do not lend themselves easily to video. Forget using video for communicating HR policy, or for explaining the latest accountancy processes. But use it for practical tasks, such as how to change a tire, or for a role play that demonstrates effective customer service.

Principle 4: Your Video Message Needs to Be Quick and Easy to Understand

People often consume media content when they're distracted, tired, or not interested. This is especially true for web video, which often competes with email pop-ups and web searches in multiple tabs on a viewer's browser.

Therefore, we must package our content so it is fast and easy to understand. If viewers don't understand our message very quickly, they will tune out. That means that for video, every picture we shoot, word we choose, or music we add must quickly get our message across. Our viewer should not be left scratching her head when she hears a word used in a script. Nor should she have to struggle to make sense of a picture we shot.

Your Brain and Video

How does your viewer's brain process the video message? If we can understand this, we can shape our message so the brain does less work and our message is understood more easily. We need to learn from both the discipline of cognitive psychology and from storytelling theory.

Cognitive Psychology

Psychologists tell us that our brain processes incoming information in three stages. These stages are known as the sensory memory, the short-term memory (also known as the working memory), and the long-term memory.

When we watch video, the pictures and sounds first hit our sensory memory, which acts like a gatekeeper. It considers if what we have just seen and heard is worth thinking about. If it's not worth thinking about, it discards it. It's a little like that expression, "In one ear and out the other," only with video, we're talking about the message coming in and out of both the ears and the eyes.

However, if the sensory memory deems what it has seen and heard to be relevant or important, it sends that information to the short-term memory. People also call this the working memory, which is probably a more helpful term, because it is where your brain works on processing information.

If the information is important enough, it will be sent to the long-term memory, where it is stored indefinitely. In the future, when that piece of information is needed, your working memory will retrieve it from the long-term memory.

How does this play out in real life? Let's say you are watching television. An advertisement comes on for dentures. Your teeth are in pretty good shape, so as the ad hits your sensory memory, you say to yourself it's irrelevant and then you forget it.

However, the next ad is for a new minivan. You have been thinking of buying a new minivan, because your dog has chewed out the backseats in your current minivan, plus you think the addition of a DVD player would be a great way to keep the kids quiet on long journeys.

So your sensory memory acts as a gatekeeper and lets all the audio and video through to your working memory, where it thinks about it. As you think about all the features—the video camera that's helpful for reversing, the DVD player to keep the kids quiet, the electric sunroof—and you compare them to the ones in your current minivan, you are engaging both your working and long-term memories. A memory of your current minivan is stored away in your long-term memory, and the visuals on the advertisement are coming in through your sensory memory to create an image of what life would be like with a new minivan. Now the more you think about the new car, the stronger the picture of its benefits becomes in your long-term memory, lasting longer and coming into stronger focus.

When it comes to the three different stages of memory, all things are not equal. While the long-term memory has an enormous capacity for storing all of our memories, the working memory and sensory memory are extremely limited. Some researchers measure capacity based on how many seconds' or minutes' worth of information each memory stage can store, while other researchers measure it in terms of chunks of information.

The academics of memory get a little complex at this point. And while the number of chunks of information that the short-term memory can store is probably a better way to measure memory, some theorists have suggested that the working memory has a time capacity of two minutes. They also suggest that the sensory memory has a capacity of about eight seconds, although you will find some theorists suggesting as little as four seconds and others suggesting as many as 12 seconds.

Three Stages of Memory and Media

What does this mean? First, you don't have a lot of time to convince the sensory memory that something is worth thinking about. In cognitive terms, your information must be short and compact enough for the sensory memory to quickly recognize its importance and transfer it to the working memory with very little effort. Within a few seconds of seeing the advertisement for dentures, your sensory memory probably discarded the ad. However, within seconds of seeing the minivan ad, it had your attention.

Second, your working memory can't think about too many different things at one time. If you give your viewer too much information, he'll suffer what's commonly known as information overload. Psychologists call it cognitive overload. So when it comes to the minivan advertisement, the advertisers promote only one or two main features of the car because they know the viewer will forget any more.

Impact on Video

The impact of this is important for all media production. It means we need to package everything in short, easy-to-digest chunks. For video, that means using uncomplicated images, short words, and easy sentences. It means not trying to put too much information or distracting irrelevancies into any sequence. It also helps us understand why complex information and stories with a lot of details do not work well in video and need to be conveyed using a different method, such as text.

Stories and Narrative

If you ask a journalist what she does, whether she works for a newspaper, television station, or radio station, she is likely to say she tells stories. That's the currency of media. Her craft is storytelling. So why are stories so important and fundamental? Human beings need to make sense of the world, and stories are our tool for doing that. Stories gather disparate information and put the pieces into an order so that we can process them.

Stories take many forms, including: history, which makes sense of events that don't always seem clear when they stand alone; gossip, which is used for entertainment and power; fiction, which allows people to escape to a world that may be a little less imperfect than our own; and persuasion, which can push people to change.

Another word for stories is *narrative*. Understanding narrative theory helps put information together in a way that's easier to comprehend. In the psychological world, narrative closely corresponds with the theories of meaning and memory. At the end of section 1, we will look at narrative theory and what it means for your learning videos.

Good videographers structure their video content so that it is a visual story. This makes it easier to understand and increases the chance of it being remembered. For learning practitioners, this should make a lot of sense, because we know that stories make learning easier and more effective.

Web Video's Relationship to the Viewer

Video can appear on many different platforms. Traditionally, popular video started as movies on the silver screen. It then spread from cinema to television. In the last decade, it has spread from television to the web and then to other mobile platforms. While this book is primarily about video on the web, we borrow many conventions from television and cinema. But our primary focus is creating video that will be watched by people who are viewing it over the Internet. They may be watching it on computer screens, mobile phones, or tablets.

Why are we differentiating between these platforms and making a big deal of the fact that web video is different from video on the big screen or television? Because media is about relationships. Primarily, these relationships are between the content maker and the viewer, listener, or reader. However, a tangible relationship also exists between the medium, or platform, and the consumer. A lot of people who lament the demise of newspapers talk fondly about holding the paper and getting ink on their fingers—this is the tangible relationship we're talking about.

For radio, that relationship has changed but has been nevertheless just as significant. In the 1940s, listening to the radio was often a group experience; people would sit around the radio and listen. Today, it's a solo experience, which makes it feel more intimate.

The relationship that listeners have has an effect on how the content is presented. For example, as radio has become more personal, the presentation style of announcers evolved to become more intimate. In the 1940s, the presenters made announcements as if a large audience was gathering at their feet. Today, radio presenters are more conversational.

When it comes to video, it's interesting to see the different dynamics of how viewers relate to each platform. People watch cinematic movies in theaters where the screen is so large and far away that they move their heads to see from one side of the screen to the other. With television, the video is across the room but is much closer, so viewers move their eyes only. With web video, viewers are so close that it is an in-your-face experience. All these differences affect how the video is consumed. The experience of the environment in which we consume the content affects us differently too. We tend to sit longer in the cinema than for television. We get up and down during television video, but generally watch a whole show.

Dimensions of the Web

With web video, most people have had enough after watching a minute or two. In fact, many don't even watch the video all the way through. The different habits of viewing video content on the web means we need to shoot our content differently than we shoot for television. This relationship between viewer and platform affects everything, from how we plan our narrative, to the relationship our content builds with the viewer, to the way we approach production from a technical standpoint. It affects what we can get away with—web video generally has lower picture quality than broadcast video.

So the platform is very important in influencing how we create and package content. The web brings some additional dimensions to how video can convey a story that never existed on the previous platforms. These dimensions are:

- the capacity to **personalize** content
- the ability to provide content **on demand**
- the capacity to create a **nonlinear narrative** structure
- the ability to deliver content on multiple **platforms.**

Personalization

Personalization is the ability to package content so it's different for each individual consumer. A good example of personalization is Amazon, which watches your purchasing habits and makes further suggestions based on what you've already shown interest in. So if you like buying DVDs of the TV series *Burn Notice*, it may then suggest you try *Leverage* or *Covert Affairs.*

Personalization can happen several ways. It can happen automatically as a program monitors your interests, like we see on Amazon. Or you can set up preferences such as daily alerts for news information. For example, on the BBC website, you can configure the settings to display the weather in your hometown, the local news, and only the local news topics that interest you.

Personalization can also be a mix of you choosing what you see and the content provider guessing what you may like, such as with Pandora radio or Last.fm. These sites ask for your general music preferences, and then stream content based on your choices.

Personalization now feels fairly standard to most media consumers. However, it has had an incredible effect on the media industry and will continue to transform how people consume content in the future. It offers exciting opportunities in learning for efficiently customizing learning content.

Personalization in video can come in many shapes and forms. It could be an immersive video experience, where viewers choose alternate endings that have been produced to help people learn various scenarios. A producer may create 30 one-minute segments of a didactic video that a viewer can either watch straight through or instead choose a selection based on their prior learning, which saves time. We are likely to see more innovative ways to personalize video. In the future, we may be able to place the learner into the video to interact with characters.

On Demand

The Internet makes content available on demand. Once again, most consumers are now familiar with this concept. You don't need to wait until 6 p.m. to watch the evening news. Log on to your computer any time you like. You may not think this is a big deal, but it affects production. Many television production techniques were born in the era when they'd shoot during the day and be back at the station to edit footage at 4 p.m. in time for the 6 p.m. news. Now that's changed.

On demand means you can watch just about any television program you want, when you want. The notion of having to stay home on a Friday night to see a program no longer exists. The BBC website allows you to watch any show for up to seven days after its initial broadcast. This means that viewers are no longer bound by the schedule. In fact, they create their own.

Nonlinear Narrative

The web has challenged the notion of a linear narrative structure. A linear narrative structure can be understood in television programming by a news bulletin. They order the story by showing the headlines and finance first, before showing sports and weather. However, the web changes all of this. You can now jump around your news program in any order you like. Skip the politics and go straight to the sports news.

Classic current affairs programs on television would bait viewers to watch their whole show (and thus see all the commercials) by constantly saying, "Coming up next. . . ." It was a neat trick that the web has done away with. We can no longer produce video content and expect people to watch from beginning to end. We cannot assume viewers will watch our content in the order we produce it, and this has implications for how we structure the narrative.

For learning, it means that if we chunk our content carefully, we can enable learners to skip content they already know, and focus on the content they need to learn, so they can make far better use of their time.

Cheap and Ubiquitous Distribution

The web has been described as a democratizing force for the media. One of the reasons is that now anyone can build their own TV channel, newspaper, or radio station. This is because the Internet connects everyone.

Fifteen years ago, if you wanted your own TV channel, you needed to apply for a license from the Federal Communications Commission (FCC). After all the effort, you then had to fund an expensive transmitter site and production facility, and then run it.

The Internet has enabled anyone to make cheap video and distribute it virtually for free to anyone anywhere in the world. And it can be distributed to any platform that is connected to the Internet and has the requisite software. It can be distributed to a PC in Chicago, Illinois; an iPad in Sydney, Australia; or a Droid smartphone in Cairo, Egypt. Such easy distribution allows a new video to be immediately available to corporate offices around the world, eliminating the waiting period associated with postal deliveries and slashing the costs of delivery. Easy distribution also changes your audience, and how your video compares to the increasing amount of video being shared.

Bolting It All Together

Video has powerful potential for communication, entertainment, news information, persuasion, and—for our purposes—education. But we need to understand how it works and how it will be viewed if we're to get the most from it. And we need to understand the process that transforms video content from a collection of pictures to a learning tool.

By considering how the brain will process our information, we are able to think carefully about how to package the content into chunks of narrative that are quick and easy to understand. When we see how it works on the web, plus the added dimensions that the web offers us for learning that take it beyond the limitations of a television broadcast or VHS tape played in a classroom, we can create more focused content that will deliver results for workplace learning professionals.

The key for new videographers who want to make video for the web or other platforms is to first think through narrative structure and then master each message layer of video on its own. Then master the process of integrating each one so your message is tight.

For learning professionals, we also need to take the video one step further from merely communicating to ensuring that video educates and helps viewers apply their learning. We've already discussed how video works. Now we need to review how learning works.

CHAPTER THREE

Video and Learning

In this chapter:

- Learning involves creating mental models
- The role of creative repetition in making learning stick in video
- Using video to create learning autonomy
- Using prior experience in didactic video
- Adding interactivity to video for learning

Using Educational Principles

How many times have you come across a video that truly transforms your understanding of a topic or that clearly teaches you the steps to follow for an important psychomotor skill? The success of the many documentary channels on cable television, such as the Discovery Channel and the History Channel, comes down to the fact that the producers package knowledge in ways that are easy to learn.

They combine good production techniques with sound educational principles. You need to do likewise to create great didactic video. Doing that requires you to not only follow the tried and tested techniques of video production that have been developed through years of cinema and television production, but also to apply educational practices. In this chapter, we will review some key learning theories that you can directly apply to video.

Now while the focus of this chapter is learning theory, it is not intended to be an extensive textbook, because there have been many excellent volumes published that you can easily consult for a more academic treatment. Instead, we're going to focus more on learning and how it applies to learning video.

For fear of oversimplifying the learning process, we might say that learning is the process of:

- showing or correcting how to do something
- making sure what has been learned is remembered
- helping the learner transfer that remembered learning into the real world.

As we go through this, we are going to look at learning from two distinct fields. The first is cognitive psychology, and the second is adult learning. As far as cognitive psychology is concerned, we'll be looking at mental models and memory retention. In terms of adult learning, we'll look at the importance of autonomy, prior experience, relevancy, and interaction.

Information Structures

If you have young children, you're probably familiar with how they report their day's experiences when they get home from school. Their stories and updates come rushing out in an excited babbling stream of consciousness that often has neither chronological nor thematic order. What they tell you does not immediately make sense. You have to slow them down and ask specific questions. It's only then that you piece together a picture of how their day went.

Until you do the work of asking questions, mentally sifting through your child's answers, and then piecing it all together, none of what they say makes much sense. And unless you're not really interested in your child's day, your brain will be working hard to make sense of everything they blurted out as they tumbled through the door, because our brains crave a sense of order. Disorderly information is not appreciated.

Our brains need to understand information and make sense of it. They like to know things, such as: how one piece of knowledge relates to another; how many pieces of information fit into the whole picture; and the sequence and timing of routines we follow that may be as mundane as loading the dishwasher, or as complex as synching email to our smartphone.

To make sense of all this, our brains create mental models that cognitive psychologists also refer to as *schema*. Mental models are helpful because while they enable us to make sense of the world, they also help us remember important information, because they are stored in the long-term memory.

Everything we understand and do is based on a mental model. Turning on the radio in your car happens because you have a model in your brain of what the on/off switch and volume control knob are, where they are located, and what button you need to press for your favorite station. When we are new to something, our brain starts building a mental model to make sense of it.

Sometimes, learners lack the necessary data to build an accurate mental model. It's like knowing that you can buy food on a flight and planning for it, but then finding out the airline doesn't accept cash, only credit cards. While you have most of the information—you can buy food on a flight—you lack some of the detail to create an accurate mental model. Learners can misunderstand the relationship between two pieces of information and end up with a faulty model in their long-term memory.

Adult educators are in the business of helping learners build the right mental models, or in some cases, helping learners correct their existing mental models. Research shows that the better organized our information is, the easier it is to process and learn. If learners already have an existing model that we can add information to, or change slightly, the learning is improved. Additionally, learning is improved when we give learners an overview before we start throwing chunks of information at them.

Producing learning video has the same goal as adult learning: to help learners create new, or correct existing, mental models. All the techniques we discuss in the following chapters—from shot size and camera angle to lighting and narrative—are the tools you have to help the viewer build a mental model.

Mental Models and Stories

In chapter 2, we talked about the power of stories in media content, whether it is video, audio, or printed. Stories are what humans use to make sense of the world, and we have been sharing them forever. Anthropologists paint mental images of prehistoric rituals around the campfire, where the earliest humans attempted to make sense of their world by sharing stories. We see early visual storytelling in ancient rock and cave paintings left by Australian Aborigines in the outback and paintings in Lascaux, France, left for ancient people from the Paleolithic period.

Human beings have always had an innate need for stories because without them, the chunks of knowledge we have about life are uncertain and lead to insecurity. Life ends up being a jumbled series of information chunks, much like the young child's rendition of his day at school. The consequence of this is that humans are already very sophisticated when it comes to stories. And very often we use story structures that already exist in our minds to make sense of the disparate information that barrages us on a day-to-day basis.

In many ways, stories are like mental models because they are frameworks that hold information together to make sense of it. Some theorists point to the fact that many different stories are basically the same plot, just dressed up differently. The classic Hollywood romance plot of boy meets girl is a good example of a plot that is the foundation of so many movies.

Theorists argue that there are a limited number of plots, and storytellers follow these to write our stories. The argument goes that many of these plots are innate. Because we were born with them, we naturally understand the story better. Perhaps this comes from the many hours of watching cinema and television, as master storytelling teacher Robert McKee suggests in his classic book on film writing, *Story*. Perhaps it comes from centuries of opera, theater, and literature. Or indeed, life experiences.

McKee lists 25 different standard genres, most of which relate to entertainment. Chip and Dan Heath have picked this up in their excellent book, *Made to Stick*, and suggested that when it comes to persuasive and inspirational communication, there are three main plots: the challenge plot, the connection plot, and the creativity plot. Each follows a narrative structure to which people relate. The familiar structure helps people put disparate information into order using an easily manageable pre-existing structure.

The power of the story is nothing new. Trainers get good feedback when they share relevant stories in their seminars that explain complex theories. Learners learn quicker when complex information is explained with analogies. We know this, and as a trainer you can probably attest to the power of story in your own practice.

Some Implications for Video

What does this mean for video? When you are clear about your video's purpose and have clarified your learning objective, think about how you will structure that learning. Can you use a story structure that is easy to remember, and that takes disparate information and puts it together in a meaningful way? When you teach knowledge, don't bolt it together as a series of bullet points. Work out its structure and then tell it as a story. And always provide a summary of that story at the outset, so your learner can contextualize the learning.

Memory Retention

Once your learner has understood your message, you need her to remember it. Cognitive psychologists suggest that when it comes to learning, we need to consider two discrete stages of memory. The first is the short-term memory, also known as the working memory, and the second is the long-term memory, where the mental models are stored. We discussed these in the last chapter.

The working memory is the part of our brain where we do our conscious thinking. It has a very limited storage capacity. Long-term memory, however, has a far greater capacity and stores all your life experiences, knowledge, skills, stories, and mental models.

Computers are not necessarily the best analogy for the brain, but you could think of your short-term memory as the RAM on a computer. (The difference being you can't upgrade the RAM in your head!) The long-term memory is like your C drive or documents folder where everything is stored. Your RAM accesses the stored information from the C drive when it works on it. And as soon as the RAM has finished with the information, it discards it by either deleting it or saving it back on the C drive. Sometimes when it saves it on the C drive, it modifies or updates it.

Repetition–Retrieval Is the Key

There are numerous techniques taught to improve your memory, such as creative visualization and associative recall. However, the best one is repetition. Remember having to learn your multiplication tables back in elementary school? You repeated them over and over again. Do you remember learning to perform a piece of music by memory on the piano at school when you were a teenager? You practiced it over and over. And not only did you remember it better, you improved your performance on stage because your memory of which notes to play was automatic and did not require much focus, enabling you to devote more of your working memory to the tonality and expression of the music.

Repetition is a key part of memory retention. That's why classroom exercises with feedback are so important along with role plays and discussion. Repetition is critical if you want people to remember your video's content. This is why television and radio commercials repeat their messages over and over. Listen to how many times they repeat the name of their product and telephone number.

In learning video, we need to find ways to repeat key learning points and do it often. The problem is that we shouldn't repeat these points in ways that make the viewer bored or send her into a trance; therefore, we need to be creative.

Creative Repetition

If your video is to train retail assistants to ask customers for their zip code when they buy a product, reinforce it by communicating the message differently each time. For example, you could include the following repetitions in your video:

1. Narrator could introduce the importance of getting a zip code at the outset.

2. Shoot an interview with a salesperson explaining how the zip code data helps the shop stock products more relevant to market demand.

3. Have a role play that prominently features a sales agent asking for the zip code.

4. Include a text graphic at the end that has the phrase, "Remember to ask for the customer's zip code."

Cognitive Load

Because the working memory has limited capacity, overloading it with too much information hinders learning and creates learner fatigue. Therefore, learning needs to be designed so it does not overload the working memory.

Create a Light Cognitive Load

One way of reducing cognitive load is to carefully structure your learning. If you're using video to help people learn a psychomotor skill, break it down as you would when doing a task analysis.

Content needs to be broken into easy-to-digest chunks of information that fit into an overall structure. Make sure you give an overview first so learners have a head start.

Another important method is to avoid distractions and digressions. Ruthlessly remove any information that is not necessary to achieve your learning objective. We often overexplain information and tend to give more detail than is necessary. Try to cut back on detail.

Also avoid the temptation to provide tangential information that might be considered "nice to have" rather than necessary. We've all been to dinner parties where someone starts sharing a story, then goes off on a tangent. They forget the original story, and we then lose track.

Adult Learning Principles

Principles of the cognitive processes that happen during the learning process are based on empirical research and help us think about how to structure video. Additionally, principles that are essentials of adult learning can help us think about how to deliver video.

The school of thinking that most professionals draw on in their day-to-day practice comes from various theories and techniques formulated by people who are now considered pioneers in the development of our field—people as diverse as Malcolm Knowles, Robert M. Gagne, Carl Rogers, John Dewey, and Paulo Freiere.

These different approaches form a group of ideas that is generally referred to as *adult learning principles*. The problem with this term is that there are numerous learning theories. Some theories contradict others. Some support them. Meanwhile, other theories are underpinned by significantly different values and opinions on the purpose of learning. It's fair to say, however, that there are a collection of adult learning principles that are widely accepted by most practitioners. Most practitioners can attest to their value through their own experience. These include autonomy, prior experience, a focused and relevant objective, and interactivity.

Autonomy

Adult learners are autonomous. Unlike school, where children have no choice but to sit through a 13-year curriculum, adults generally do so because they are motivated to learn. With autonomy comes self-direction. In an ideal world, adults would set the direction of their learning, the pace at which they would complete their learning, where they would like to complete it, and in what chunks.

Yes, we do not live in an ideal world. Budget, staffing, and schedules all conspire against attempts to create true learning autonomy. But the principle for adult learning is to create as much autonomy as possible. This means the trainer, teacher, coach, or consultant is actually seen more as a facilitator than as a curriculum director or learned professor. She facilitates the learner's journey and adapts to meet the learner's needs.

Malcolm Knowles, a pioneer in adult education, says that adults are often driven by internal motivation, such as increased job satisfaction, improved self-esteem, and a better quality of life. Of course external factors can motivate learning too, including career promotion, salary increase, and the quest for a corner office. What does this mean for adult learning practitioners? It means we allow the learner to direct their learning and respond to their needs at a time that suits them, rather than impose our assumptions on their learning needs.

Some Implications for Video

When we use video to create learning, it is helpful to follow these principles:

Avoid the temptation to create a 30-minute documentary. Instead, give your learner the choice to watch the whole 30 minutes in sequence, or break it into mini-segments that stand alone and can be watched by dipping in and out.

Make your video available across different platforms so people can watch it on their computer, laptop, tablet, or mobile phone. That means thinking about how the picture will look when viewed on a phone or tablet, as opposed to the average computer desktop screen.

Prior Experience

Adult learners are different from children because they bring prior experience to a learning situation. If you are running a workshop on organizational change for adults, they are likely to bring with them experiences of either having led an organizational change process or having been changed. And with these experiences, they are also likely to bring some opinion or philosophy of dealing with that change.

School children do not have these experiences, and therefore their education is about giving them foundational data to consider. Adult education is about drawing data from learners' experiences and processing it to form learning.

What does this mean in a learning situation? Facilitators first should not assume that their learners know nothing about the topic. This assumption clashes with more traditional approaches to education, where a professor is assumed to "know all" and the student is an empty vessel waiting to be filled with knowledge and learning.

In adult education, the first step is to identify that knowledge and experience and then draw on it in the learning process. Use that experience to frame theories or learning. Recognize that finding prior knowledge and experience can also mean skipping parts of a curriculum, because the learner already has that expertise.

Some Implications for Video

Be explicit about what each video covers. Mention your learning objective at the beginning. If your learner already knows what you cover in the video, she can save time by moving on to another, more relevant video.

Don't always assume your viewer is ignorant about what you cover. Instead, offer a link to assumed knowledge. For example, to understand how to export a Word document as a PDF, you should have some knowledge about file formats. So instead of cramming repetitive information about file formats into a short video about making PDFs, assume your viewer has this knowledge. But offer another video about file formats for viewers who don't have this knowledge, and provide a link to it.

Goal-Focused and Relevant

Adult learners come to a class or workshop with goals. They generally know why they are taking the class and how it will achieve their goals. Adult learning theory suggests that learners don't just come to a class to have fun. They attend because the knowledge and skills they learn will help them achieve their goals.

What does this mean for learning practitioners? It means being clear on what their class is about, clearly identifying the learning objectives, and helping the learner link the class to her goals. For example, if participants attend a workshop on leadership communication, the facilitator will make sure the learner can see how the objectives will help her as a leader, and will help show how to solve particular situations she is dealing with or may face in the future.

Some Implications for Video

Make sure the title of your video describes what people will learn from it. If possible, work your learning objective into the title. If all this is too much, make sure the learning objective is clearly described or listed so viewers can quickly determine if your video is relevant to them.

Provide a short description of your video that explains why your learner needs to watch this video, and how he can apply the new knowledge to his work.

Clearly communicate how long the video will last and what time commitment the viewer must make to follow it.

Interactivity

Adults learn and remember better when the content is delivered in an interactive format. People are less likely to remember a long lecture than an interactive exercise or discussion. Learners draw on their experience and wrestle with what the theory and their experience means for them.

Of course we know from cognitive theory that this is because learners are engaging the working and long-term memories, which improves retention through repetition. We also know that lecturers battle with keeping the attention of students for all sorts of reasons, and learners are most likely to give their full attention to activities in which they are engaged.

Some Implications for Video

Create a workbook that mirrors the video and directs the learner to take notes. By writing it down, they are repeating it. Provide some stimulus information and summaries to avoid cognitive overload.

Provide exercises in the workbook so the viewer can pause the video, complete the exercise, and then return to the video. That way they don't end up in a trance watching the screen.

Plan interactive elements into your narrative structure so that viewers can choose what's next. Remember the books where kids could choose their own adventures? Why not create a "choose your own adventure" sequence for learners? For example, "Click here if the boss accepts feedback and click here if she doesn't." You've then created alternate scenarios. This is harder work and requires more careful planning of your narrative structure. However, it can be rewarding for topics like safety and leadership.

Video Offers Powerful Opportunities for Trainers

Video is an ideal instructional tool that offers many opportunities to present learning in ways that are easy for learners to understand, remember, and apply. To get the most from it, trainers should draw on their skills as instructional designers to break down information into digestible chunks, create a narrative structure for these chunks so each chunk is easy to understand, and include creative repetition of key learning points throughout their content. Following the key principles of adult learning, video should be made available to learners on demand, giving them the flexibility to watch it in an order appropriate to their needs.

CHAPTER FOUR

Video in Practice

In this chapter:

- Using video for organizational learning
- Producing video in organizations
- High-end versus cheap and cheerful
- Organizational impact
- Future of didactic video

Using Video for Organizational Learning

More people than ever are using video as part of their organizational learning strategy. But specifically what part of their strategy? And what's motivating them to use video rather than face-to-face seminars or synchronous online solutions? Apart from the obvious reasons to reduce corporate demand for costly and timely travel to training on the other side of the country, there are some strong pedagogical reasons.

Anders Gronstedt, from the Gronstedt Group in Colorado, who has been producing learning video for clients for more than 10 years, now creates television quality webisodes for large companies to help facilitate organizational change. Adopting a mockumentary style, like in the hit TV show *The Office,* his clients release bi-weekly webisodes that encourage conversations among staff about key corporate issues. Video has become an essential tool for influencing the change process.

American Airlines creates short knowledge chunks in video and embeds them into online learning solutions that staff can access when they need them. The videos are also embedded into standard PowerPoint slide decks that trainers use in face-to-face training to better illustrate routine but detailed tasks.

For example, one of their online learning modules looks at how to disassemble a seat in an aircraft's first-class cabin.

Learners can click on parts of the seat to watch a video that shows the specific actions required for that part of the seat. It's learner-directed because the learner can look at the component she needs to see rather than watching a whole video, when only a fraction may be relevant to her current needs. It's self-paced because she can watch it as many times as she likes. But that's not the only value of learning video.

Traditionally, learners in a classroom have had to crowd around an instructor and other students to watch the process over his shoulder. The video camera can take the learner in very close to see the task performed at different angles, which creates perspective and brings the object to life. Embedding video is a great way of integrating the power of video with other learning delivery mechanisms.

Some organizations use video as a way to communicate organizational issues and keep staff current with company news. Carter Knox is senior vice president of Human Resources at A&P Supermarkets based in New Jersey. He is a veteran in the area of staff development and communication with a great track record in the retail sector. He's used video for the past 20 years at a number of companies where he's held executive positions, including A&P and OfficeMax. "We've used video as an integral component of corporate communications to directly and quickly communicate to associates," he said. He's created corporate news shows, executive messages, strategic vision pieces, financial updates, and critical bulletins.

While a lot of learning video has been about broadcasting content to staff, more companies are looking at how to make video a shared two-way experience. Jiffy Lube, the automotive services chain, has been using video innovatively to do just this. It started when trainers from the company's corporate university were given small cameras and were asked to collect the company's success stories on video along with ideas and experiences from staff. Jiffy Lube University launched JLU Tube, which got an amazing 6,500 hits in its first week. Surveys found that 80 percent of viewers were interested in submitting their own videos to share. Learners even suggested topics of learning they'd like videos on. So video is morphing from just disseminated content to evolving conversational content that is being shared. Jiffy Lube's learners are typically 18 to 25 years old and are very open to social media, but as learners become more and more sophisticated with new technology, we'll see learning open right up.

Anders Gronstedt challenges how we approach learning and suggests that we are bogged down in our thinking. "Frankly, a lot of instructional designers design really boring video," he says. "They're stuck on the classroom metaphor and try to replicate a classroom. The classroom never really worked in the first place. We have to move beyond that and use new metaphors, such as television shows."

Television shows are a great metaphor to be inspired by. But there are more metaphors that will push the envelope: for example, coffee shops and pubs where people learn through conversation. Imagine a social video site within an organization where technicians share videos of how they solve problems in much the same way they may troubleshoot when a bunch of colleagues go for a drink after work.

Different organizations are motivated to use video for many reasons. These include influencing organizational change, providing specific skills training, disseminating information across a workforce, and encouraging staff to participate in building learning.

Not all didactic video looks the same. Some video learning professionals use drama to achieve their objectives. After all, storytelling, learning, and influencing are closely linked. Others use a newscast format to share information because it's effective and familiar to audiences. And some use video to build customer scenarios, walk through sales situations, conduct interviews with subject matter experts, and send leadership messages.

Sometimes the video content is independent and stands on its own, while other times it may be integrated into face-to-face solutions, online learning modules, and mobile tablets.

Producing Video in Organizations

As the cost of production decreases, more and more companies are building in-house teams to do videography. Some are training learning practitioners to create video as part of their learning roles. Others continue to hire outsourced video professionals.

Carter Knox has set up several in-house production teams to deliver communication and learning video products of a high production standard in large retail corporations. "Installing an internal production house does involve a good deal of up-front cost," he says. "But once the investment is made, the equipment and staff quickly pay for themselves over the high cost of using an agency."

Setting up an in-house production facility takes time, and members of staff need to be trained to use the equipment, write scripts that exploit all that video as a medium has to offer, and create content that is easy to understand, remember, and apply. Often you can find people already experienced at this, but many times companies will train their staff with these new skills. Along with buying equipment and training staff, solid processes need to be set up for managing media assets, developing content, working together as a team, and managing the internal client process. Without processes to guide these, and a disciplined approach to following the processes consistently, the operation is in danger of being folksy rather than professional, and punching below its weight.

Not every company goes for a high-end production house approach. Jeff Tillet is a strategist and evangelist at Float Mobile Learning, where he works with organizations wanting to enter the mobile learning space. Jeff has used both high- and low-end video production tools in his instructional design work over the past 10 years at Food Services America, Microsoft, T-Mobile, and now Float Mobile Learning. But he's enthusiastic about the opportunities offered by lower end equipment for nonprofessional videographers—namely the trainers—to shoot practical video that aids learning.

"We had a higher end studio at T-Mobile which was used heavily, and we couldn't always schedule time in the studio," Jeff says. "So the learning and development folks established a budget to buy prosumer equipment, and we started to produce our own training videos." He suggests there's a level of equipment for everyone. "You could buy a Flip camera that has HD or use an iPhone 4S. You don't have to spend $5,000 for a camera. You can basically do it for any budget." Jeff encourages people to shoot video that is natural and raw, because it's fast and efficient as well as effective. It also puts a powerful technology into the hands of the trainer. More and more organizations are equipping their training teams with the skills to produce quality educational video on a shoestring.

The Association for Energy Affordability, based in the Bronx, NY, has rolled out training in low-end video production to its entire learning team and some members of its field staff. "Staff are taking cameras out into the field with them during energy audits," Director of Curriculum Development and Accreditation Anna Sullivan says. "They are becoming more involved in the production of video."

The association teaches classes on weatherization to clients across the country. Access to video cameras enables trainers to capture real life examples of what they teach in class, making the face-to-face learning experience more real. They are also using the footage in their delivery of synchronous live video learning sessions. "More staff are being involved in this and I can see video production skills being a necessity for trainers in the future," she said.

Using trainers to capture video footage is only one part of the association's overall video strategy; the organization also maintains a video production unit staffed by two former television professionals who produce higher end video, so the organization is getting the best of both worlds. There's a real tension between those who believe video should be shot by professionals and those who think anyone can produce video with their iPhone 4S or FlipCam.

"We do the whole thing," Anders Grondstedt says. "Professional video crew, professional director, professional actors." Grondstedt's crew doesn't churn out simple how-to-videos, but rather complex dramas with actors delivering a carefully planned narrative. "One of the biggest mistakes is to use real people rather than actors," he says. "Real people have no clue how to act, even if re-enacting things they do in their everyday work."

It's hard to disagree with Grondstedt when it comes to drama-based video. Drama is complex work and requires an advanced level of skills. However, for other forms of video, learning professionals who are trained to understand the dynamics of video and develop the necessary production skills to create good content will work well. At the end of the day, there's no right or wrong—it's about knowing the level of quality you want.

High-End vs. Cheap and Cheerful

So what's the best level of production to aim for? The kind of "wobbly-cam" that's poorly lit that you see a lot on YouTube? Or the smooth, polished video that looks like a network television production?

As technology has developed and people can shoot video without investing in large cameras, more and more people are going for less polished video. In fact, in some circles, more polished, highly produced content is even viewed suspiciously, while others suggest it's simply distracting. "In learning, spinning logos and fancy intros are not always needed," suggests Jeff Tillett. "We're not expecting broadcast-quality video," he says."So embrace that. Embrace the aspect that it is done low budget and have fun. Have that be part of your story. When you're having fun, you make a connection, so people will smell that." Embracing that earthy realness is all about the content.

It's the steak rather than the sizzle that makes content useful for learning. And this is borne out at Jiffy Lube University, where video shot by staff who are not video professionals is getting great reviews. In their user survey, 95 percent said they would return to watch more video.

It's hard to take a stand on either side of the debate. It probably comes down to your organization, your audience, and the purpose of your video. One thing is clear, though: Many of the professional production techniques used in television can be applied to low-end cameras, and following these will get you good results.

Organizational Impact

Video is hot at the moment. More and more organizations are looking to make it a part of their learning strategies. The drawback to its popularity is that it may be seen by some as a fad. Perhaps it is. Whether or not it's a fad, however, organizations are seeing good results.

Mike McCauley is a senior program developer in American Airlines' Maintenance and Engineering Training Group. He and his colleagues shoot their own video using basic video cameras and get excellent results. "Video lets you be at the location of whatever you are doing.

Commercial aircraft are extremely large and complex machines to understand. You can use a video to bring the person to it."

Carter Knox, who has been using video for the past 20 years, has seen the direct benefit of video. "Operational videos in particular have helped drive performance," he said. "A couple of organizations that I have been at have created 'Manager On Duty' training videos for retail stores." The videos provide a visual walkthrough of tasks the manager must perform on a daily basis. "They clearly displayed the expectations that associates needed to execute upon which allowed the organization to create controls to keep them accountable."

Knox has seen video both change attitude and increase knowledge. "We used a video to create an understanding of what our company's brand meant. Associates began to live the brand because they could see it. Part of video's power is its ability to affect emotion. Organizations I've been part of have used video to subtly and carefully drive change."

Anders Gronstedt's work creating mockumentary webisodes has had significant organizational impact. The drama series he created for his client's sales teams made explicit the behaviors the organization wanted from their staff by personifying them in characters in the webisodes. "Typically we have a scenario when one character is steeped in an old way of selling and someone else does it better," he said. "We're finding in organizations that people will make reference to these characters. They will say, 'I don't want to be like Bob.' We create really strong characters to embody the message of the training." Gronstedt adds the secret: "It's all about storytelling—you tell effective strong stories. That's how we all learn."

"We launched a new episode every Friday," Grondstedt said. "And people were following it like they were following a TV show." To create real buzz within the organization, they also launched an audio podcast every other week that was based on a radio talk show format. The actors would call in to the show in character and maintain Facebook pages.

When video is used innovatively, it has huge potential. The challenge, Gronstedt says, is to see learning beyond the metaphor of the classroom.

Future of Didactic Video

One of my favorite quotes from Marshall McLuhan is that we're in danger of driving forward looking in the rearview mirror. He was talking in the 1950s about the birth of television, but his wisdom is especially relevant today as video becomes a powerful tool for learning professionals. Back then, television producers created TV shows as if they were stage shows because theater was their metaphor. With the powerful tool of video, what is our metaphor?

Clearly, video technology is accessible to everyone. Unfortunately, when you buy a camera, it doesn't automatically confer to you the skills of a videographer, despite all the bells and whistles on some of today's cameras. But these skills can be learned, and with discipline we can become competent videographers. But what does this mean for learning?

"The big rage this year has been gaming," Anders Gronstedt says. "And looking at various game applications, I can't say we've really cracked that in terms of integrating games with video. But I think that's an area where we're going to see more and more growth."

Mobile is also a key part of the future too. "Mobile is a fantastic medium for video," Jeff Tillet says. "I constantly watch videos on my phone. Video can be incorporated in apps and mobile-enabled websites." Tillett has worked on mobile content to accompany learning curricula, so learners can practice and reinforce what they learned elsewhere via the phone.

The iPad has also opened up exciting possibilities for learning to both display learning video and shoot it to share. Video will be an important part of the social learning space as we look for more engaging ways to build learning relationships.

Predicting the future is a dodgy practice because so much can change. Virtually no one predicted YouTube, Twitter, Facebook, or their successes. It's safe to say, though, that video will be a tool that's used to stand on its own or will be incorporated into other learning delivery methods.

Section 2:

How Video Works

One way to understand video is to see the different elements as a series of message layers that build on top of each other. The better you understand each of these layers, how they help the brain process information, and how they work together, the more control you have to create really powerful content.

Video message layers include, but are not limited to: pictures (the video footage); visual effects (graphics, filters, transitions); spoken word (commentary, monologue, and dialogue); music (soundtrack); and sound effects. In each chapter of this section, we will go into more depth about how to control each of these message layers to achieve your video's learning objective.

If you look at video through the framework of message layers, it becomes easy to understand how to increase your control of the video message, as well as how to plan your content. Each message layer has a set of basic rules you need to follow to ensure that your message is quick and easy to understand. You need to learn these so you can ensure that each layer packs its maximum punch in conveying your story.

By understanding video as a series of message layers, we can start to think clearly about every single element in our video. This gives us more control to manipulate the overall message and ensure that it is targeted to meet our learning objectives.

CHAPTER FIVE

The Picture Layer and Visual Grammar

In this chapter:

- The language of video
- Importance of regularly changing shots
- Drawing a storyboard
- Balancing context and intimacy
- Moving the camera
- Setting the camera angle
- Camera placement
- Conveying meaning through the background

Pictures First

As soon as you have determined your learning objective and completed a task analysis, you need to think about what pictures you will use to demonstrate your learning. It's tempting to start with your written script, but thinking through the pictures first will make your video far more powerful and memorable.

If you're used to conveying information in writing, such as in a report or user manual, working with pictures can be difficult at first. That's because pictures are their own language and have a complex grammar that we need to learn. This visual grammar is the result of many years of experience in cinema and television where pioneers have tried different ways of telling stories with pictures.

This chapter is about how to use pictures to tell your story. These conventions will help you create a powerful storyboard that is then easily transferred to a script, and enables you to capture some powerful footage. Among other things, we'll look at how to frame a shot, select the right background, and influence who looks more powerful in the shot.

Moving Pictures Are Worth Three Thousand Words

Next time you find yourself in an airport, try this informal anthropological study. Head to one of the bars and look for business colleagues traveling in pairs. You'll find some chatting over a beer. Most airport bars have television screens on the wall where you can see either CNN or a sports channel. And just about everyone in the bar will be within eyesight of the TV screen.

Now, watch the interaction between the two people you have targeted. Who is doing most of the listening? Watch where the listener focuses her eyes. Is she focused on her traveling companion or the TV screen over the bar? Most of the time, you'll find her watching the TV screen as her companion rattles on.

This is the power of video. Pictures are a magnet to the eye. And in almost every situation, they'll trump other communication methods such as the humble conversation. Pictures are the bedrock of every video message. With pictures, your video has life. With too few pictures, your video message will be lifeless.

Skilled videographers start planning video by planning pictures. In practical terms, this means drawing a storyboard before writing your script. (Novices tend to write scripts first before scurrying away to find pictures that match the commentary or dialogue.)

Most of us have heard the phrase, "A picture is worth a thousand words." So much can be told visually. And when it comes to video, we get even more words for free because we get to see the complete action and various nuances associated with it.

However, pictures often don't tell the whole story. For example, a picture of a traffic jam tells us clearly that there is a traffic jam. But it doesn't say where, when, why, or who is in the jam.

As powerful as pictures are, they're a little like Swiss cheese—they have lots of holes. We need something to fill these holes in our message, and this is where additional message layers come in. When we shoot video, we rely on video to tell as much of the story as it can before then looking to other message layers to fill in the blanks.

The Language of Video

Back in elementary school, when you were taught to write, you were taught that a paragraph is made up of sentences, and that a sentence is made up of words. Your success as a writer came down to how well you put words together in a sentence, and how well you put sentences into a paragraph.

Each individual word is identified with a set of relatively simple meanings. When you see the word *walk*, you have a good idea of what it means. The word *walk* is a signpost to the concept of walking. A combination of words, such as a sentence, creates a more complex meaning. For example, the phrase "walking briskly" creates a richer message.

Pictures are a language too. So when you tell stories in video, it's much the same. Except instead of using words, each of which carries its own meaning, you use shots that also carry meaning to piece together your message. Everything we do tells a story. If you see me limping, you know I hurt my ankle. If I smile, you know that I am happy.

Like a sentence, we need more than one shot to make our message clear. For example, when you see me smiling, you have no idea why I am happy. But if you then see a shot of me licking a nice big ice cream cone, then you know I'm happy because I had ice cream. Instead of building meaning using words, we are building meaning using pictures. And while we will also use music, sound effects, and the spoken word to create the overall message in the video, viewers will primarily use the pictures to understand your message.

So if verbal language has words, sentences, and paragraphs, what does video have? The smallest unit, equivalent to the word, is the shot. A **shot** is a single piece of video footage. It could be someone smiling. It could be someone skiing. And just as words make up sentences, shots make up what we call a **sequence**. Just as your sentences make up a paragraph, your sequences make up a **scene**.

We're talking about a language. So if, like most people, you were trained in the language of spoken and written word, you now need to learn a new language: pictures. How does all this work? Consider the following sentence:

> Michelle pulled into the parking lot to meet her colleagues, but as the minutes ticked by, she grew anxious that no one else was going to join her.

Shot one: wide shot of Michelle's car driving into parking lot. (photo by Amanda Anderson)

This makes sense in print. If we were to tell this story using video, we'd need to think carefully about different shots that convey the same message. To the right are pictures that show how we might describe the story in words that we will then create visually.

Shot two: close-up of Michelle looking anxious. (photo by Amanda Anderson)

As a communication medium, video is primarily pictorial. People remember your pictures more than what has been said. That's why when we are in conversation and a nearby television is turned on, our eyes are almost always drawn to the television rather than the person we are talking to. So the first thing you need to do when planning video is think about which shots you need to create a visual sentence. Then it's a matter of crafting each individual shot so it carefully conveys your message. To do this, you need to think about shot size, camera movements, camera angles, where you place your camera, and what background you use.

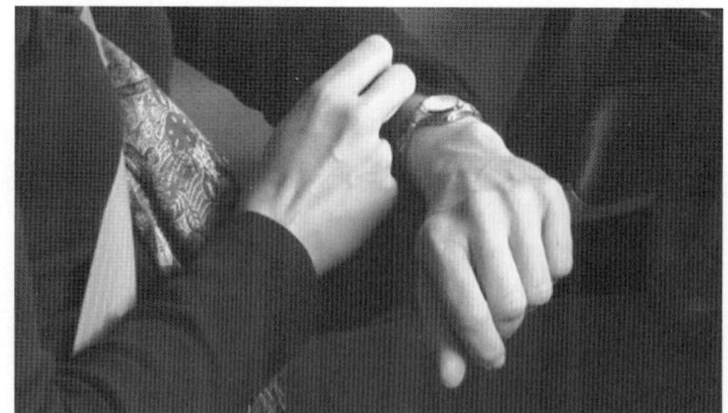

Shot three: close-up of Michelle looking at her watch. (photo by Amanda Anderson)

Changing Shots and Shot Sizes

People are drawn to pictures. Does that mean if you simply plonk your camera down, press record, and capture all the action that people will be riveted to the screen? Not quite. To keep your video interesting, it needs to be made up of many different shots. To understand this, imagine that you're sitting on the porch of a house somewhere in suburbia, reading the newspaper and sipping a cup of coffee.

Your neighbor across the road starts mowing her lawn. The instant she takes her lawn mower outside, your eyes will be drawn from your newspaper to her as she starts the engine and then pushes the mower across the grass. Your brain processes the fact that she is cutting her grass, but after a few seconds, you go back to your newspaper because it gets boring. You don't spend the next 30 minutes watching her cut the grass.

This same behavior takes place when people watch video. If there's only one shot, the viewer tends to lose interest within a few seconds and his mind becomes distracted. This is why videos of lectures don't work well. They put a camera in front of someone giving a lecture and don't change that shot for a whole hour. Within seconds, their viewers are struggling to stay interested.

If you watch television news, you'll see that broadcasters hardly ever show an entire press conference. And even if they spend a whole five minutes on that press conference, they don't hold the same shot for more than 10 to 20 seconds. While the audio of the press conference runs, they cut to a shot of the politician's hands, a shot of other journalists in the press conference taking notes, and then to different angles of the politician as he talks.

To keep people interested in your shots, you need to plan a sequence of different shots. This makes them interesting and engages the viewer. How long should you hold a shot? Unfortunately there is no set answer, because every shot is different and decisions about length need to be made on a case-by-case basis. You should really hold the shot only as long as you need to get your message across. In practice, aim to change your shot regularly. If appropriate to your story, change every four to 20 seconds.

Given the need to change shots regularly, let's reconsider the pictures we used to describe Michelle driving into a parking lot to meet colleagues who don't turn up. Visually, we expressed this with a wide shot of her car driving into the parking lot. Then we had a close-up of her face to show that she was concerned. To express the fact that things were running late, we featured a close-up of her watch.

Let's consider the action itself when she drives into the parking lot. The act of driving in and parking her car would actually take 10 to 20 seconds if we filmed it in its entirety. Do we really need to spend 20 seconds of our viewer's time to simply express that she was driving to a parking lot? No. The viewer would quickly lose interest. So we need different shots to express the fact that she is driving into a parking lot in order to ensure that the viewer doesn't lose interest.

By starting with the original shot of Michelle driving into the parking lot, with the camera positioned so we show her car actually in the road, we have an establishing shot. We could add a shot from inside the car looking over her shoulder as she drives in. Then we could change the camera's position so we see her driving into the parking space itself. Then, of course, we still shoot pictures of her looking anxious and then checking her watch.

This is an interesting sequence that will keep the viewer's attention. By cutting between these shots, we can also save some time, so the sequence of her coming into the parking lot actually takes less than 10 seconds. This is how it would look.

Shot one: wide shot of Michelle's car driving into parking lot. (photo by Amanda Anderson)

Shot two: inside car, over the shoulder as Michelle turns into parking space. (photo by Amanda Anderson)

Shot three: wide shot of Michelle turning into parking space from the front. (photo by Amanda Anderson)

Shot four: close-up of Michelle looking anxious. (photo by Amanda Anderson)

Shot five: close-up of Michelle looking at her watch. (photo by Amanda Anderson)

You may be thinking that this seems like a lot of work, for just 10 seconds of video. It is. But that's the reality of video production; it takes time. However, if we don't take the time to get these extra shots and make the sequence more interesting, our viewers will not take the time to watch our videos.

You might also think that cutting between these different shots looks staged and unnatural. If you watch television, you will see they constantly cut between different shots, and it looks very natural. The reason is that the editing is professional, and you'll learn more about that later.

Even if you think that this makes sense, you may be scratching your head wondering how to apply constant shot changes to didactic videos, such as lectures. In fact, people often ask me how to make a standard and generally boring lecture more visually interesting. Actually, I think that's the wrong question. The correct question is, Does a typical lecture lend itself to didactic video? Remember our four core principles of video? The first principle is that if there's no action, don't waste your time producing video. Granted, there are times when you will have little choice but to shoot the lecture because your boss has told you to do so or because you simply don't have the time or budget to do something more effective. However, try to avoid lectures if you can.

Generally, we talk about shots in terms of sequences. Sequences make up a scene. A sequence could be someone walking through a door, which involves several different camera positions. Or a sequence could be someone making a phone call.

Draw a Storyboard

The first step in planning each sequence is drawing the storyboard. A storyboard is a visual representation of the planned shots, usually a series of frames with drawings in them for each shot. Under each frame, you will include additional details such as camera angle, movement, or shot size. Your storyboard does not have to be a piece of art—many people merely draw stick figures—but it does need to be easy to understand. Please see the example of a storyboard on the following page.

Scene: Michelle & Parking Lot

SHOT SIZE: WS – Michelle pulls into
CAM DIRECTIONS: parking lot Camera is stationary
COMMENTARY/DIALOGUE SUMMARY:

SHOT SIZE: OTS inside car as
CAM DIRECTIONS: Michelle turns wheel
COMMENTARY/DIALOGUE SUMMARY:

SHOT SIZE: WS Car pulls into
CAM DIRECTIONS: parking space Cam at front
COMMENTARY/DIALOGUE SUMMARY:

SHOT SIZE: CU Michelle looks
CAM DIRECTIONS: around with anxious expression
COMMENTARY/DIALOGUE SUMMARY:

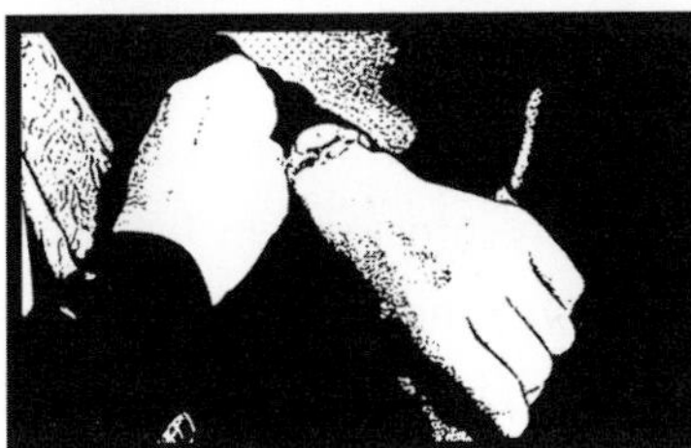

SHOT SIZE: CU Michelle rolls up
CAM DIRECTIONS: sleeve to look at watch
COMMENTARY/DIALOGUE SUMMARY:

SHOT SIZE:
CAM DIRECTIONS:
COMMENTARY/DIALOGUE SUMMARY:

Once you have planned your shots, you can start planning the other message layers to fill in the gaps or build out the story, with spoken words or music. Having drawn rough sketches of each shot, you can more quickly identify what else you will need. Will commentary be necessary to convey your message? Will music help create a particular mood? Are any special effects needed?

Once you have finished your storyboard, the next step is to write your script. We talk about how to write the script in chapter 9. You can also give a copy of your storyboard to anyone who might shoot or edit the video. This will give them a visual sense of what you're aiming for.

It's tempting to skip drawing a storyboard. Some people like to "wing it" by leaving every shot to chance. They turn up on location and make up the shots as they go along. This is risky because they have little time to think about things like the 180-degree rule, where to position the camera, and what cutaways to gather. Failing to do a storyboard almost always guarantees more time in the editing process. It also raises your chance of shots that don't cut together, which adds more stress in postproduction. And often, because of a failure to plan, you miss important shots because your attention is torn in too many directions.

Spending the extra time to think carefully about where you will position your camera, what angle you'll set it at, and what shot size you'll use gives you greater control over your picture and leaves less to chance. Visualizing helps you plan your props and background, minimizing the risk of mistakes. It will also save you time in the field and will lead to less uncertainty. A storyboard forces you to think these things through and trains your brain to become more visual.

Time and time again, I've seen people save significant time by starting first with a storyboard. And they have almost always come up with better results. The one time a storyboard is not good is if you have no idea what you will be shooting. You want to avoid this situation. However, if someone says, "We need you to shoot an interview in five minutes while the CEO is visiting the plant," you'll have no choice, in which case you should fall back to the five-shot or three-shot formulas we discuss later.

Shot Sizes—The Balance Between Intimacy/Detail and Context

The video camera is your viewer's eye. When you place your camera in front of a person, you are effectively putting your viewer in front of that person. The closer you place your camera to that person, the more intimate and personal the relationship is between your viewer and that person, and the more detail you get to see. It's just like real life. Conversely, the further you place your camera from your subject or object, the less intimate your message is, and the more it becomes about context.

We describe the level of intimacy or context in terms of shot size. Shot sizes range from close-ups to wide shots. Like a lot of language used in film, television, and now web video, there is some variance in terminology. It can depend on whether you work in TV or film, or in one country or another. We use the term *wide shot* here, but some people use the term *long shot*. Wide and long are interchangeable in video.

Planning each shot size in your sequence helps you think through your pictures so they best convey your message. Using the language of close-up and wide shot makes it easier to work in teams. If someone else is shooting your video, you and your colleagues can use the same language to ensure that you are working to create the same effect. If you are hiring a professional videographer, this is the language they will use.

What are the different shot sizes? Let's start from intimate and work out to context.

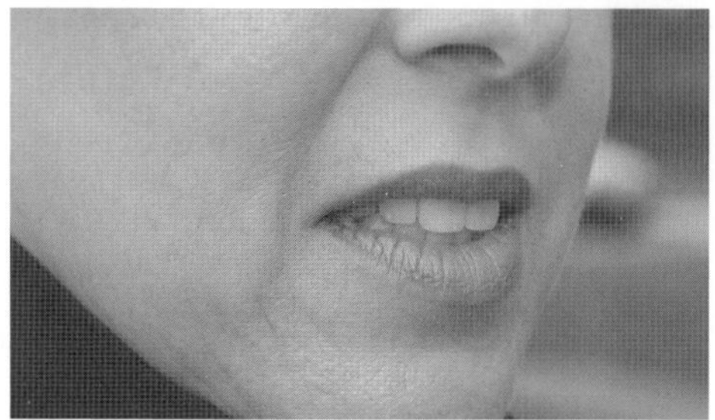

Extreme Close-Up (XCU)—The XCU focuses on a tiny detail on your subject or object. Sometimes known as a macro shot from its use in the still photography world, it is as intimate as you can get. It is not a very natural shot and should be used sparingly. It can also highlight smaller visual aspects that are key to your message. For example, in this shot, the XCU is of the actor's mouth and shows concern. In educational video, an XCU can bring into focus a small detail that is relevant but difficult to see with the naked eye.

Close-Up (CU)—the CU is your standard intimate shot that shows personal emotion and helps create a connection between the viewer and the subject. It usually runs from the head to the shoulders and shows little of the person's body language.

Mid-Close-Up (MCU)—The MCU keeps the subject's emotion in focus but brings in a small portion of body language, as it captures your subject from the top of their head to the area around their shirt pocket. In this shot, you start to see some of the background, which gives context, although it's really about the emotions of the person in your shot.

Mid-Shot (MS)—The MS is where both context and emotion are of equal importance. Body language comes into focus and is more obvious than emotions, as this shot generally runs from the top of the head down to the subject's waist.

Mid-Wide-Shot (MWS)—Your MWS is where body language is most important. You don't see the detail of emotion on your subject's face or in her eyes. But you can see whether they're confident, slouching, or ready for some sort of action. The MWS is good when you need to include two people or even a group in the picture, because you can see the relationships and dynamics within the group.

Wide-Shot (WS)—In the WS, you see your subject from head to toe. You also get a good view of the context that the subject is in: in this case, an inner city park just after the leaves have fallen in November. The WS is too far away to see emotion, but it is good for establishing shots. The WS is also good for shots with more than one person.

Extreme Wide-Shot (XWS)—The XWS is generally your establishing shot and shows the spatial and geographic scale of where your story is set. For example: an inner city park during fall. Your subjects may be in the shot but are probably not. If they are, they may be so small that they're hard to recognize, and their presence will have little impact on the story the picture is telling.

Over the Shoulder (OTS)—The OTS is a close-up shot of an object or your subject that is shot from over the shoulder of someone else. If your shot is of a person, the shoulder over which the shot is taken generally belongs to the person your subject is talking to. It is useful for dialogue between two people if you are doing a role play, and for interviews with subject matter experts where you would shoot over the shoulder of the person doing the interviewing. An OTS can also be used to show point of view.

Camera Movements

When shooting video, you may find yourself moving the camera to create interest. There are four main camera movements you can use. These are: tracking (also known as trucking), zooming, tilting, and panning.

Tracking Shots

Tracking refers to a type of camera move in which the camera itself moves. There are two types of tracking shots. One is tracking "in" or "out." The other is tracking "left" or "right." Tracking shots are sometimes called trucking shots.

The term comes from cinematography. Cameras are placed on a dolly that glides up and down a small portable railway track, which is set up on location. This railway track eliminates the bumpy motion of someone walking while holding the camera and enables the shot to move smoothly.

Dollies and tracks are not cheap. Nor are they quick or easy to set up, especially in some shooting environments. To get the same effect of smooth movement, camera operators will often use steadicams. Steadicams were introduced in the 1970s and are a harness that the camera operator wears over the shoulder and anchored around the waist. This harness holds the camera in a way that separates the operator's physical movement from the camera, so the camera can move smoothly without picking up the operator's movement. The operator can walk and get a tracking shot that is almost as smooth as if it were on a dolly rolling on a railway track.

In electronic news gathering and corporate video, camera operators tend to use shoulder-mounted cameras, which gives them more balance to hold the camera without wobbling. Tracking shots are difficult with cheaper hand-held cameras because the cheaper cameras are lighter and more difficult to hold steady, unlike professional cameras, which are shoulder-mounted and are heavier.

Track Left or Right

Tracking in and out refers to a type of move where the camera moves in closer to the object or subject, or moves farther away. It is also known as a dolly movement and trucking.

Tracking left or right refers to moving the camera left or right. It's also known as crabbing and trucking because crabs move sideways.

Zooming In or Out

Zooming in and out are sometimes confused with tracking in and out because it's a camera move used to bring the viewer either closer or farther away from the subject. While the moves are similar, the effect is different, because tracking involves physically moving the camera, and zooming involves adjusting the focal length of the lens.

Zoom In or Out

Unfortunately, zooming is overdone today. As a result, it has the potential to look like the work of an amateur, so use it sparingly. There are two other reasons to avoid zooms. First, they do not appear smooth when streamed over the Internet. Second, nonprofessional cameras tend to have very cheap zoom controls so that when you zoom it tends to happen too fast and is jerky, unless you have a very steady and gentle hand. Professional cameras have more expensive controls that enable a smoother zoom.

Tilting Up or Down

Tilting up or down is the movement when you change the camera angle while the video is still rolling. "Tilting up" means rolling the tape as the camera moves from low angle to high angle. "Tilting down" is when you move the camera from high angle to low angle.

Tilting shots are often used to create a sense of power. For example, positioning your camera on the ground outside a skyscraper, and then slowly tilting up, can emphasize how high the building is.

Tilt Up or Down

Panning Left or Right

When you move the camera from left to right, you are **panning**. The actual movement takes place as if your camera is on a vertical axis and your camera moves horizontally. Shortened from the term *panorama*, it is an effect that enables you to capture a majestic scene.

Pan Left or Right

Panning works very well in cinema but works less well on the web. This is partly because it is overused by amateurs, so it looks somewhat folksy. Pans also tend to appear jerky rather than smooth when streamed over the Internet because of bandwidth and compression limitations.

Simulated Movement

Video producers are often faced with visual material that does not move, such as photographs. This creates a dilemma because movement is necessary to create visual interest, and simply showing a still photograph will lose the viewer's interest. To create the sense of action, the camera operator shoots an extreme close-up of the photograph and then pans across the picture, creating the sense of a real-life pan. This technique has been popularized as the "Ken Burns effect" because he used it extensively to give historic still photographs more life on the screen.

Using Camera Movements

It can be very tempting to use camera movements. However, be cautious and really ask yourself if you need these camera movements. Web video makes it difficult to display movement smoothly. Some may also argue that you shouldn't need camera movement, because the action in your shot should include all the movement you need. Also, just about every home movie and wedding video shot by a family member is full of dizzying zooms and pans, so there's good reason to be cautious.

So when should you use camera movements? Ask the simple question, Does this movement add to the narrative? Are you moving the camera merely because you can, or to reinforce your story?

Camera Angle

We said earlier that your camera is effectively your viewer's eye. Wherever you place your camera, you put your viewer. That means that when you put your camera at a certain angle, you are positioning your viewer either below or above the object in your video. Camera angle has two purposes: It determines the power (either in the relationship between subject and viewer or in the status of the subject in relation to other subjects or objects), and it creates interest. There are four types of camera angles. They are eye level, low angle, high angle, and bird's-eye.

Eye Level—Eye-level shots create equal status between the viewer and the subject. They take place when you position the camera roughly on the same level as your subject's eyes. It's best to place the camera ever so slightly below the eyes, but not so much as to notice it. Eye-level shots are important for interviews, presentations, and any situation where you want to create a natural rapport between the subject in your video and your viewer.

Low Angle—Low-angle shots are where you position the camera below the eye level so the camera is looking up at the subject or object. This shot makes the subject feel bigger and gives the subject the power, while possibly diminishing the viewer. These shots are used to convey confidence, power, and control. Low-angle shots are great for training videos, when you want to make the boss or leader easier to identify.

High Angle—High-angle shots are when you position the camera above the eyeline so that it is looking down at the subject. It makes your subject look smaller and diminishes their power. It makes your subject appear weak and powerless. You might use a high-angle shot in a video about workplace harassment to convey the victim's feeling of helplessness.

Bird's-Eye—A bird's-eye shot is when you are looking down at the subject or object from above. It is the classic helicopter shot, and not very common for training videos because it's an expensive shot to get and is more artistic than functional. It's also very unnatural because we don't often look down at subjects or objects from such height.

Using Camera Angles

Camera angles offer you all sorts of opportunities to use the visual picture to tell your story. But like any tool, the power of camera angles comes from your ability to both use this technique wisely and execute it with subtle precision.

A common mistake is shooting low-angle shots of people that are so far below the eyeline that they are exaggerated and look ridiculous. These shots simply become a caricature and distract from your message. It's easy to do the same for a high-angle shot, and position your camera so high that your subject looks ridiculous. When viewers start noticing your camera angles rather than following your story, you have failed.

Camera Placement and the 180-Degree Rule

When you plan your storyboard, think carefully about where you will place your camera. Some videographers tend to wing it when it comes to camera placement, and this can make things difficult further down the line when it comes to editing.

It's always a good idea to scout your location before drawing your storyboard. This way you can work out in advance where you'll place your camera.

For example, if you are going to shoot someone walking out a shop door, will you place the camera so it faces the door head on, from inside the door, outside it, slightly to the left of the door, or slightly to the right? How does that position work when cutting to the next shot? Your decision will either make your sequence easier or more difficult for your viewer to understand.

One of the classic rules of film and television that applies the same in the new world of web video is the 180-degree rule. The rule simply states that you draw an imaginary straight line across the ground where you are shooting. You then position your camera on one side of the line and don't cross that line.

Imagine you are shooting a sports event and draw a line down the center of the field from one end to the other. The 180-degree rule suggests you put your camera on one side of that line and never cross it. If you keep crossing the line, you will be crossing from one side of the field to the other. While one minute your favorite team is shooting goals to the left of the screen, they start aiming for the right of the screen when the camera crosses the line. This makes it difficult for your viewer to keep up with the action. So the convention is to keep all cameras on one side of the line.

This rule makes it easier for your viewer to know who is who, and prevents him from being disoriented. The rule also works in situations like interviews. If you are conducting an interview, always keep the interviewee on one side and the interviewer on the other. If you are doing the interview in several sittings, it can be easy to forget this, and then you make it more difficult for the viewer.

If you have two experts speaking in your video, perhaps debating opposing viewpoints, make sure you shoot them on opposing sides. Once again, this makes it easier for your viewer to follow.

Context—Your Background

While it's important to think about what is happening in your shot, it is also important to think about where it is happening. Your background can help tell part of your story. Likewise, it can undermine your story if you don't take care.

One of my clients asked me to critique a series of corporate videos. One video featured company executives talking about their corporate vision. My client shot the video at a hotel because they all happened to be meeting at a hotel conference center one week, and it was a great opportunity to get them all in one day. However, he shot the head of operations talking about streamlined manufacturing efficiencies while standing in front of a piano. He chose the location because the light was good. What does a piano have to do with streamlined efficiencies? Nothing. The piano was irrelevant, distracting, and undermined this executive's credibility.

Think about where your action takes place. Look at the backdrop. How does it reinforce what your subject is doing? In the case of my client, he should have shot the executive while she was standing on the plant floor.

It's tempting to find a backdrop that has a smart aesthetic quality to it. While this is good, make sure your backdrop also reinforces your story. If someone is talking about workplace safety, shoot their commentary in the workplace. If you're talking to an academic, shoot them standing or sitting in front of a bookcase. You get the idea.

You may think this is cynical and leads to stereotyping. In a way it does. But the reality is that the brain generalizes everything as it sorts through the information to make sense of the world. So having a dentist wear a lab coat and sit in his dental clinic helps you more efficiently convey your message. It saves you adding in commentary that "this man is a dentist."

Summary

Creating didactic video is more than just pointing your video camera and hitting the red record button. Successful video is always well planned, starting with a storyboard that shows how each shot fits together to convey your message and describes how it looks. Your storyboard is the blueprint for whoever picks up the camera and shoots the video, and is the basis for writing your script.

As important as drawing a storyboard is, knowing the rules of visual storytelling and the practical terms of production is also essential. The grammar of video will ensure that your video is easy to understand, and using the video terminology will focus your planning and make the production process more efficient.

CHAPTER SIX

The Visual Effects Layer

In this chapter:

- Transitions
- Filters (or effects)
- Graphics

Enhancing the Pictures

Everything tells a story. If a man is limping along the road, it tells us that this person has a disability or injury—perhaps a sprained ankle or sore toe. While it's true that everything tells a story, it's also true that everything doesn't always tell the whole story. Why is this man limping along the road? Was he in a fight? Did he trip over a cable?

This is why we have multiple layers in video. Each layer works in combination with other layers to ensure that the whole story comes across. Once you have assembled the pictures you need to tell your story, you can look for other message layers to tell the part of your story that the pictures have not been able to tell. Then, once you have filled in any holes, you will also look at how to add more power to your story using different layers.

Visual effects can add power to your narrative. Often, they can convey changes in time: a translucent dissolve can create the effect of a flashback; a message can be exaggerated by manipulating colors; an action can be emphasized with a slow motion render; and a viewer's attention can be captured with transitions.

Sometimes visual effects will make our pictures more explicit and tell more of the story. These effects can be simple graphics, such as were used in the 1960s *Batman* series, where directors cut from action shots in fight scenes to full-screen stand-alone graphics with colorfully illustrated words such as "Biff" or "Bam." Or these effects may transform the original image, like converting modern footage into black and white, or overlaying a traditional film grain effect so it looks like the action was shot 80 years ago.

In this chapter, we look at how you might use the visual effects layer to give your video more power. As a learning practitioner, you are likely to use one of the three types of special effects in your learning videos. The key to using special effects is to use them sparingly and only when they will add to your message. A common mistake among novice filmmakers is to use fancy transitions that are garish and distract the viewer from the story. Used well, they'll subtly build on the pictures to enrich your story.

Transitions

Transitions refer to the way you change from one shot to another. You will be familiar with transitions because you have probably seen them used in PowerPoint slides. Traditionally, television editors would cut between shots simply and without fancy transitions. However, increasingly, they are incorporating transitions and effects to act as punctuation marks in the narrative. For example, the television series *Burn Notice* often splits the screen into several boxes with shots of Miami to separate parts of the narrative. In shows like *Burn Notice*, the transitions have become part of the visual look and feel of the program, which is important in entertainment video. But fancy transitions are less important in learning videos, where the purpose is helping a viewer learn a topic quickly and easily, as well as making it easy to remember and apply.

Transitions are added into your video when you cut the shots together in the editing package. Windows Movie Maker has a range of transitions, as do iMovie and virtually every other editing package. You can also buy transitions as plug-ins for advanced editing packages. You'll find transitions such as starbursts, flashes, barn doors, portals, zooms, and many more.

In all reality, you will find little reason to use most of the transitions. Many are flashy and serve little narrative purpose other than to draw attention to your whiz-bang technology. There are probably very few narrative purposes for a starburst transition or a venetian blind transition. For learning videos, stick to simple cuts and cross-fades unless it reinforces your learning.

In this example, the venetian blind transition distracts the viewer from the narrative. When cutting between the shot of one woman at her desk and another woman at a different desk, the transition does not help us understand the meaning any more than simply cutting between these two shots. It only distracts us as our brain asks what's going on.

Shot one

Transition

Shot two

But when used carefully, they can aid your storytelling. Let's imagine you have two shots in a video sequence. The first shot shows a woman sitting in her office behind a desk, sending a text message on her phone. The next scene features her on vacation skiing down a mountain in Colorado.

Shot one: Nicole in office.

Traditionally, you would cut between these two scenes. A simple cut, however, may not be appropriate. In fact, it may help your story to use a transition that carries some of the narrative. Let's say you want to suggest pictorially that this woman was daydreaming about her skiing vacation in Colorado. To create the flashback effect of daydreaming, you could use a transition that transforms the image so it loses focus and goes blurry, and then sharpens up on her in Colorado, skiing down the slopes.

Transition: Blur effect.

Transitions come in all shapes and sizes. Consider carefully how they will add to the narrative.

Shot three: Nicole skiing in Colorado. (photo by Shutterstock)

Effects and Filters

Video effects, also known as filters, change your picture. Like transitions, you generally add these filters during the editing stage. Some cameras, however, offer the options of filming with certain effects, like black and white. For maximum flexibility, never use the camera to add special effects, and always shoot your video normally. It's easier to transform a color video into black and white than make a black-and-white video into color. Video effects can do a number of things. These include converting your pictures, correcting the quality of your pictures, and altering your images.

Using filters and continuing our earlier example of the office worker daydreaming about her vacation, we could manipulate the second shot (of her skiing) and make it look washed out, or even convert it to black and white to further reinforce the fact that it is a flashback.

Convert Your Pictures

Hundreds of video effects and filters are available to today's videographer. While many are built into your editing program, many more can be bought as plug-ins. Filters can do all sorts of things, such as add a film grain, or convert your frame rate to 24 frames per second so it looks like it was shot on traditional film.

Correct Your Pictures

While some filters will convert your pictures, others will fix them up. Let's say you forgot to set your white balance when shooting your video. You can add filters that make the appropriate adjustments in the editing package. Other filters will allow you to sharpen your image or add further color saturation.

Alter Your Pictures

You can buy video effects to plug into your editing software that allow you to adjust the appearance of someone's face. For example, an innovative plug-in from NewBlueFX can smooth out wrinkles and soften skin tone. Others will take your standard video footage and transform it into an animated cartoon.

Effect: Animation.

Add Background

An exciting video filter that comes with a lot of consumer-level editing packages today is chroma-key, better known as blue screen or green screen. Chroma-keying has been around for years and allows you to shoot a subject or object in front of a blue or green screen. The computer replaces everything on the screen that is green or blue (depending on whether your back screen is green or blue), with an image of your choice. This gives you the power to shoot in a studio and then insert the picture of your choice behind you. If you want to appear at the beach, it's as simple as replacing the background image. TV weather broadcasters commonly use chroma-key technology and have the meteorologist stand in front of the green screen while superimposing the weather map behind.

In theory, doing chroma-key is easy. But in practice, it is finicky and takes experience to really look good. For example, if you don't light the green screen correctly, it becomes hard to insert a backdrop, because the backdrop may have what's known as hot spots, which change the gradient of green. The green needs to be perfectly even across the whole screen. Other problems include having your subject stand too close to the green screen. This can make it difficult to separate the subject and the green. Sometimes, when not lit properly, a neon blur forms around the subject. The latest version of Windows Movie Maker (Windows Live Movie Maker) doesn't have green screen capability built in, but you can find it in the advanced options of Apple's iMovie.

Caution About Filters

Filters give you a lot of power over your picture, more power than television producers had a decade ago. But there are some downsides. Applying them so they don't look fake takes skill and lots of practice. If you overdo the process of smoothing out the wrinkles on someone's face, their skin can look so smooth that it is unreal.

Adding effects also slows down your production time. It's all very well to add green screen, image sharpening, and color saturation to a shot. But displaying and rendering this image takes a lot of processing power by your computer. Many people with loads of effects find themselves leaving their computer on overnight so it can take the eight or nine hours necessary to render the final copy.

Graphics

Graphics are the images you insert into or overlay onto a video sequence. Graphics come in all shapes and sizes. Generally they are independent shots (either still or animated) that are cut into your video, or in some cases overlaid on top of it. Graphics include pictures, graphs and diagrams, captions, and animations. Graphics are very common in television—think of the weather forecast. Graphics are effective at conveying information and concepts fast and easily. They are also valuable in learning videos.

Animated graphics are more sophisticated, and enable you to do many things, such as show action in steps over time and create fancy visual motions. You can create graphics using programs like Adobe Flash or Adobe After Effects, export them as video files, and then bring them into your editing package.

Pictures

Pictures are straightforward. They're simply photographs or hand drawings that you use to illustrate your topic. Sometimes you will use photographs because you are unable to get video footage. If you are using more than one photograph, change it regularly so you don't lose your viewer's interest. Avoid holding it onscreen for more than eight seconds. Alternatively, use the Ken Burns effect to create the feeling of movement.

Graphs and Diagrams

Graphs are used a lot in television news for stories on finance. They include pie graphs, bar charts, and line graphs. Graphs are only good in video if they convey essential information, so be selective when using them. If you use graphs, make sure they are not complex. Video is not good for conveying complex information. Instead, keep them very simple and focus on one message at a time.

Imagine you're looking to convey the fact that your company has an increasing number of people who will retire in the next five years, but has a very small number of recruits from Generation X. You also want to represent the perceived loss of knowledge as these folks retire. Don't cram it all on one graph. Create separate graphs for the number of retirees in the next few years, the number of younger recruits, and the measure of knowledge to be lost from the business.

The same principle goes for diagrams: Keep them simple and make sure you don't try to cram too much information into the diagram. Use fonts that are large enough to read but not large enough to be overbearing. Think carefully about how they will appear on a computer screen and the screen of a mobile phone if people will view them outside the office. Choose a sans serif font over serif fonts, and ensure that there is a high contrast between the font color and the background.

If you're making simple web video on Live Movie Maker or iMovie, you can get away with creating your graphics in PowerPoint or Keynote. If you're using a higher level editing package like Final Cut or Premiere, you should create graphics in Photoshop or CorelDRAW, and export them as high-quality images so they render in high definition. When you create graphs and diagrams, follow the rule of thirds, which we'll learn about in section 4.

Captions

Captions are also known as lower thirds and Astons, or Chyrons. They're the written content that appears at the bottom of the screen during an interview and gives the interviewee's name. Make sure everyone appearing in your video has a caption with their name and a reason for being in your video.

When you create captions, go for simple straightforward captions. Their purpose is to tell the viewer the name of the person and their title. Some people use animated captions where the text flies in from the right, does a double somersault, and then rests at the bottom right of the screen. These are nice and fancy, but how do they help the narrative? Usually, they are distracting.

Like creating graphics, you can generate captions in your editing program or import captions as a PNG transparency. (Note: For Movie Maker or iMovie, it's best to generate captions within the program.) If you plan to import the captions, you can easily create them in Photoshop. When you create captions, always choose a sans serif font. Solid, square fonts are best because they're easier to read and do not pixelate on the screen. Compare these two examples. The first features a caption in Times New Roman, a good font for print. However, it does not look good onscreen, and it isn't as easy to read as the second example of a sans serif font, Franklin Gothic. Avoid fancy fonts, because they're distracting and not always easy to read.

Caption in a serif font does not look as strong onscreen.

Caption in a sans serif font is easier to read.

Make sure there is high contrast between the font color and the background. For example, if you have a light background and your font is white, it will be hard to read against the backdrop. Sometimes you have to use a light color because that's the office standard. If this is the case, add an outline or a shadow effect behind the text so that the light text stands out. Or create a dark box behind the caption and put the caption on top, so it's easy to read.

Do not cram too many words into your caption. Hold the caption onscreen for as long as it takes to read it twice. If you have two lines for the caption, make sure you don't put too much of an explanation into the second line. Remember, this is not television. Your video is likely to be viewed on a small screen, and depending on bandwidth, the resolution may be low.

This caption has too much information.

This caption has just enough information.

Animations

Animations are simply pictures that move and are not video footage. They could be a diagram, cartoon, or special effect. This book is about creating fabulous web video, fast and affordably. So there's a good chance you won't be investing in special effects.

Generally, special effects are created in Adobe After Effects or Flash Professional. Special effects can be anything from transmogrified shapes that form into words or pictures, to cutaway animations that show how an airplane is manufactured. If you have the luxury of commissioning or even creating animations, ask yourself first how the animation will tell your story.

Summary

Visual effects add an additional message layer to your pictures and can be used to correct poorly shot video. With today's software, you have so many options to alter the original video or correct it that it is easy to produce very sophisticated content. However, with all the bells and whistles, fancy transitions, and plug-ins that create weird and wonderful effects comes the temptation to use effects more than you need. Overuse of visual effects can distract from the narrative and is a sure sign of an amateur. Excessive use of effects, especially when you rely on them to correct poorly shot footage, adds time to your production and slows down rendering. (This can be easily avoided by making sure your footage is shot correctly.) Try to use visual effects sparingly and only when they support your narrative.

CHAPTER SEVEN

The Spoken Word Layer

In this chapter:

- The importance of writing to pictures
- Writing for the ear
- Adopting a conversational tone
- Choosing the right words
- Writing phrases
- Laying out your script
- Implications for learning

The Supporting Role of Words

If you work in a corporate environment, you know how important it is to never undermine your boss publicly. If she is giving a presentation that you prepared for her, you don't draw attention to the contribution you made. As far as the message is concerned, she's the boss and it's her job to share it. Your job is to support the message. A similar relationship exists between the spoken word layer and the picture layer. Pictures are the boss and the spoken word plays a supporting role, albeit an important supporting role.

The spoken word layer consists of commentary, monologue, and dialogue. Commentary is spoken by a narrator, unseen by the viewer, who reads the script out loud over the pictures. They tell the story interspersed with action or dialogue. This is typical in documentaries and industrial videos. A monologue is where a character in the video speaks both to the camera and over pictures. Monologue tends to be more introspective and is often used by a character sharing her thoughts in the first person, much like a Shakespearian soliloquy. Dialogue is where several people in your scene have a conversation.

The spoken word generally adds detail and specifics that pictures sometimes lack. For example, a picture of people sunbathing at the beach might convey the fact that it's summertime. However, the spoken word may add details like: "It was the hottest day on record," "It was the last day of summer," "Vitamin E is good for your health," or "Skin cancer is increasing at alarming rates." It's interesting how we need the additional message layer to really focus the message.

The first mistake people make when writing the spoken word is that they rely on the spoken word to carry the bulk of the message. This usually happens if they write their script before drawing the storyboard. The second mistake is writing as if their material is going to be read, not heard.

Writing to Pictures

If your pictures must do the heavy lifting, not the spoken word, then the role of the spoken word (like music and sound effects) is to tell the parts of your story that the pictures cannot. Words are there to add power to the pictures, not to explain or repeat what is obvious in the picture. If you have a picture of a woman walking in a park who sits down and then bows her head, the picture does a pretty good job of telling us about what is happening. But it does not tell us why she is bowing her head.

We don't know why this woman's head is bowed. The spoken word can add this information.

Is she stressed out and taking time away from the office? Is she praying? Is she doing yoga exercises? We can't tell, so we need another message layer to fill in the gaps of information.

A narrator could read the following commentary: "Take a break in the local park to relieve your stress."

Here, pictures and the spoken word work together. You'll note that the commentary complements the picture with additional information to complete the story, but it does not repeat what is already clear in the picture—Michelle is sitting in the park with her head bowed.

Writing commentary that does not repeat what is in the picture is a technique known as writing to pictures. It assumes that the spoken word is secondary to the picture. If you've ever written scripts for podcasts or radio, you may find yourself tempted to ensure that there is no silence. This comes from the need in radio and audio podcasts to avoid silence, which is known as "dead air."

When it comes to video, dead air applies to the whole package—sound and visuals. So as long as you have pictures that convey your message, silence is OK. In fact, if you can get away with a picture and no spoken word content, your video will be more powerful. This is what Alfred Hitchcock meant when he said the purest form of cinema was the silent picture.

Writing for the Ear

Writing spoken word for video follows many of the same principles as writing podcast and radio scripts, with the exception of not repeating what's obvious in the picture. Shortly, we'll look at methods that make your scripts easier for your viewer, but first, let's put some context into why these methods work.

We know that when your viewer's brain first sees and hears your video, she will triage the information in the sensory memory, deciding whether or not to pass it into the working memory. Your sensory memory, which has an extremely limited capacity, will make this decision very fast. Because the working memory has a limited capacity too, we need to reduce the amount of work the viewer does when thinking through the message.

Heavily detailed graphics, lots of distraction within the video picture, and elements like poor lighting put more pressure on the viewer's brain to figure out what's going on in the video. In addition to this, the more work they do to try to understand your commentary, the greater the cognitive effort. In a nutshell, complex sentences that are not easy to immediately understand make it more difficult on your viewer. Therefore we need to make everything in the video easy to process. For the spoken word, this means making sure every word and phrase are not complex, but are quick and easy to understand when they are heard out loud.

That way, your viewer's brain is not spending her energy deciphering your message, but is instead considering your message. Great teachers make the complex seem simple. That's also the job of video communicators. Here are three aspects to focus on when you write your script: tone, words, and phrases.

Tone

The spoken word is best understood when spoken in a conversational tone. If you follow writing conventions that were taught in high school, your message will sound wooden and overly formal on video. It will also take your viewer's brain more time to process your message. Some of the grammatical conventions that work for written English can be sidestepped when it comes to the spoken word. This, of course, raises some eyebrows among the grammar purists, so it may be helpful to review the role of grammar, especially in regard to video.

Grammar is a set of rules for communication. The rules ensure that we are efficient in our communication and that, as much as possible, people aren't left scratching their heads trying to understand someone's message. When we follow the rules of grammar, our message should be quickly and easily understood, because our method is efficient and consistent in the manner we share information.

I see grammar like road rules. Just as road rules are designed to keep traffic flowing, grammar is designed to keep the information flowing and to reduce cognitive load. However, like road rules, grammar can sometimes create inefficiencies. If you're stuck at a traffic light at 2 a.m. waiting for a green and you're the only car in sight, the red light is annoying and plays no role in safety. This is a great example of where the road rules actually cause inefficiency. However, during peak hours with hundreds of cars buzzing through, having no traffic lights would be mayhem.

When it comes to the spoken word layer, there will be times when you ignore traditional grammar and decide to run a red light. That's OK if breaking that rule makes the message quicker and easier to understand. In my experience,

I've found many people new to media start writing their scripts so they are painstakingly correct in their observance of grammatical rules. It actually makes the message slower and more difficult to understand. The purpose of video scripts is not to get marks for grammar, but to make the message immediately accessible to the viewer.

So, how should you write? First, write your script as if you're speaking to your viewer. Write in the present tense and use contractions, because that's how people speak every day. Use similes and metaphors your audience will immediately understand, because this draws on existing mental models and speeds up your message transfer.

Be cautious, though, if you have an international audience. For example, sporting terms such as "stepping up to the plate" are great, especially for American audiences. While most baseball, basketball, and football terms are quickly understood by Americans, many do not make sense to people living in Europe or Asia. The better you know your audience, the easier it will be to choose the perfect metaphor to help them unlock your message. For example, you might have a better impact in Commonwealth countries if you use cricket terms, and in Europe if you use football (or soccer) terms. For familiarity, make sure you communicate the way your audience does. Avoid technical jargon unless your audience is a technical audience. Avoid colloquialisms that your audience will not understand.

Words

Back in elementary school, you were probably encouraged to discover new words. When you handed in an assignment, the more complex words you included, the easier it was to score an A. If you wrote, "I decided to perambulate the park," instead of, "I decided to walk through the park," you would have received extra marks from Mrs. Jones.

Now that we've grown up, we don't need to impress teachers with fancy words. Adults impress people with their ideas. The words they choose are merely tools in the process to help people understand ideas. In the world of media, our purpose is to ensure understanding as quickly and easily as possible. That purpose must influence our word choice.

The key to finding the best words is to choose simple ones. Please note we're not suggesting simplistic words that treat our audience as if they are ignorant. No. Simple words. So instead of saying *commence*, we would say *start*. Instead of *conclude*, we'd say *end*. Here are a few rules to follow when choosing your words.

Favor shorter words over longer ones. Shorter words are quicker for your viewer to process. That's why "end" is better than "finish." It's why to "buy" a ticket is better than to "purchase" a ticket. People often joke about the use of monosyllables in media because they're associated with dumbing people down. Monosyllables don't dumb down the message; they make it quicker and easier for people to understand. (When the message has been dumbed, it's usually been dumbed down well before anyone chose the words.)

Favor several short words over a longer, more complex word. "Walk through" will be more effective than "perambulate." Listen to how these two words sound. "Walk through" has two syllables and "perambulate" has four, which slows down comprehension.

Use words that are familiar. Most people won't immediately know what "perambulate" means. Why create unnecessary cognitive load for viewers when they'll immediately know what "walk through" means?

Choose words your audience uses. A common mistake in HR and corporate videos is the regular use of MBA-type jargon. Apart from alienating some people and raising cynicism in others, it slows down comprehension. Is there a time when jargon is appropriate? Yes—only when you know your audience has sufficient expertise to immediately recognize and understand it.

Use visual words that carry emotion. The more visual the word, the more effect you will have. Obviously you need to think carefully about your audience and what is acceptable to them. But consider the following three words that have similar meanings: reduce, cut, and slash. Reduce is very neutral so when you say, "reduce spending," it has little emotional quality. If you say, "cut spending," you'll have more emotional quality. If you say, "slash funding," you have both emotional value and the visual quality of slashing, which gives more personality to the sentence. *Cut* may be more appropriate than *slash* for some audiences, so use judgment. But make sure your words have some visual and emotional value to them.

Choose words that are easy to pronounce and have an even tonal quality. Are they easy for your commentator to pronounce? And do they sound good? If you have the name "Bureau of Meteorology" in your script, and your commentator can't pronounce it clearly, it slows down comprehension and distracts from your message. Find another word or set of words, such as "Weather Bureau."

Also, the sound of a word is important in word choice too. Some words have greater phonetic qualities than others that make them sound better. If you know who will narrate the script, think about how they speak and form their words. Do they have any unique tonal qualities that suit some words more than others? Do they have any vocal traits that you should write? For example, if they have a lisp, never end phrases with words that end in s.

Summary

- Choose shorter words over longer words.
- Favor several short words over a longer, complex word.
- Use familiar words.
- Use words your audience will quickly recognize.
- Choose words that carry visual and emotional value.
- Choose words that are easy to pronounce.

Sentences and Phrases

Many of the conventions that make the written word rich and interesting are not appropriate for spoken word content. For example, subordinate clauses and quotations give a written sentence life. When it comes to video and audio, however, these techniques require your brain to do more work and therefore slow down the comprehension process. Here are some guidelines for writing your phrases.

Keep your phrases as short as possible. This should not be a total surprise. The shorter the sentence, the quicker your viewer's brain will be able to process it. Look at your sentences and ruthlessly chop out any word that is not necessary for conveying your message. Sometimes when we get stuck in a rut, we use words that sound great, but when removed from the sentence, they make little difference. Look at your script and interrogate each word: Do you need it? If you take it out of the sentence and the meaning does not change, leave that word out.

If you're used to writing for print, you may feel bound to follow the traditional sentence structure of subject, object, and verb. Don't. Sometimes, when your picture is telling most of the story, all you need is a word to complete the message. A great place to see examples of this is in cinema advertisements.

Ensure that each phrase has just one clause. Subordinate clauses lengthen your sentence and increase cognitive load. If your commentator narrates a sentence that has a subordinate clause, your brain has to park the first clause while processing the subordinate clause before remembering it when the subordinate clause finishes. This is extra work, and it slows down cognition. Invariably, subordinate clauses can become their own independent clause.

For example, avoid: "The divisional restructuring process, although not well planned, reduced costs by 20 percent." Instead, say something like: "The divisional restructuring process was not well planned. However, it reduced costs by 20 percent."

Using two independent clauses enables our sensory memory to quickly pass the first clause into the working memory. The working memory, as we discussed in chapter 3, has the capacity to hold more information than the sensory memory. So we need to avoid having long sentences with more than one clause, because they bog down the sensory memory, creating a bottleneck.

Write phrases in the active rather than passive voice. The rules of Plain English favor the active voice because it tightens sentences and brings the identity of the actor into focus. It works just as powerfully in spoken word media.

Basically, active and passive voice refer to what comes first in a phrase: the actor or the action. A passive voice sentence will place the action before the actor. For example:

The restructure was ordered (action) by the CEO (actor).

In this sentence, the action was ordering and the actor was the CEO. If written in the active voice, it is as follows:

The CEO (actor) ordered (action) the restructure.

Not only is the active voice more direct, but it also saves words, which keeps sentences nice and short.

Favor verbs over nouns and abstract nouns. To give your spoken word energy, avoid gratuitous nouns and opt for strong verbs. Abstract nouns will slow down comprehension. They tend to involve more words and sound less tight. Here's an example of a sentence with an abstract noun: The president started a process of negotiation with Congress to achieve budget cuts.

You can tighten this phrase and save six words by saying: The president negotiated budget cuts with Congress.

Avoid adjectives and adverbs that can be more powerfully expressed with pictures or another message layer. You might want to say, "It was horribly hot as Juan rushed to submit his application before closing time."

However, by planning a close-up of Juan sweating in the heat, you can avoid the need to say he was horribly hot and simply say, "Juan rushed to meet the application deadline."

Check that your phrase sounds correct. Often we will write sentences on paper that are clear when we read them, but are ambiguous when spoken. This is because we often run words together when we speak them.

For example, if you read the phrase, "Government concerned over rising attacks on senior citizens," you quickly understand the message. But say it out loud and it can also sound like "a tax" on senior citizens. This is why it's very important to read your script out loud to make sure every phrase is clear before you record it.

Avoid quotations. Quotations give life to a sentence in print. But they are unclear when heard out loud. Consider the following phrase: The CEO said, "I am making every effort to find jobs across the organization for people who are affected by the outsourcing of the HR division."

No matter how you read this, the narrator must become an actor when she reads the direct quote. This never sounds good unless the actor is a world-class impersonator. When you face quotations, you have one of three choices: you can have the actual person record that quote and insert it in your video; you can hire an actor to perform the quote convincingly; or preferably, you can paraphrase the quotation. So it could be: The CEO promised to make every effort to find jobs for people affected by the HR outsourcing.

Summary

- Keep your phrases as short as possible.
- Keep each phrase to one clause and avoid subordinate clauses.
- Write in the active rather than the passive voice.
- Favor verbs over nouns.
- Avoid adjectives and adverbs in commentary.
- Check that your phrase sounds correct.
- Avoid quotations.

Lay Out Your Script

There are many ways to lay out your script. It is more important for you to make sure your script is easy for you and other people working on your video to read than it is to follow one layout convention. Hollywood and television drama scripts follow a different set of layout conventions than documentaries, news, and industrial videos. In Hollywood, for example, one page of a script generally equals one minute of screen time. Folklore has it that Hollywood veterans can guess the length of a screenplay by how heavy the script is. Because of the pressures of filing stories for deadlines, TV news reporters often don't work with scripts at all—they write commentary freehand on scraps of paper in the editing room, once they have seen the pictures and how they cut together. It's here they fill in the gaps with the spoken word.

But if you're making didactic video, you're most likely to follow a documentary format when laying out your script. These generally have two columns. The left column describes the action and the right column contains the script for spoken word content, plus any audio. (Some people will include the audio in a third column.)

Your script will look something like this. When you create your script, double-space the spoken word commentary so it's easy to read.

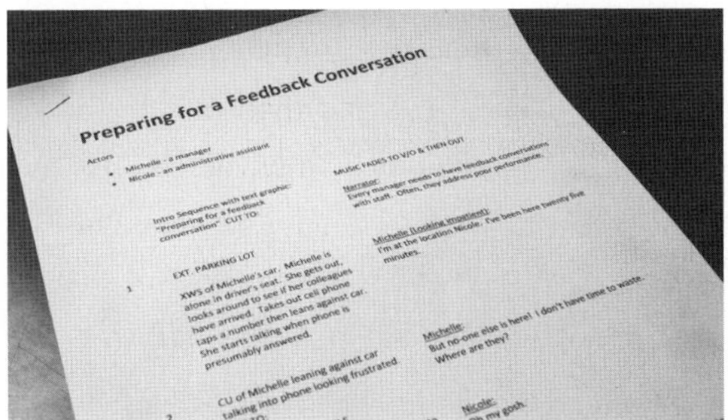

This is an example of a script in a two-column format.

Spoken Word Layer

The spoken word layer plays a vital role in the storytelling process. It supports the pictures by carrying additional information that the picture fails to convey. When you write commentary, monologues, or dialogue, adopt a conversational tone, using language your viewer will quickly and easily understand. Choose simple rather than complex words and keep your phrases short. Allow your pictures as much room as possible to speak on their own, before adding the spoken word.

The Music and Sound Effects Layer

In this chapter:

- How music affects the viewer
- What to use music for
- The power of sound effects
- Legal issues with music and sound effects
- The option to create your own music

Influencing Mood and Energy

While the spoken word layer adds detail, the music layer will affect your viewer's mood, emotion, and energy. Once again, it should add to your picture, not repeat it. Both music and sound effects are two tools that add emotion to the message and expand the sensory impact of the story. While music constitutes a different message layer than sound effects, each one fulfills a different storytelling purpose, and we're going to look at both of these in this chapter because there are some crossovers.

First we'll look at each message layer, review the legal aspects, and then look at where to find music and sound effects for your project.

Music

Music is an important part of everyday life. Some people sing along to music when they sit in traffic. Others dance to it. Others use it to relax and change their moods, while some people use it only as a background noise. All kinds of music mean many things to different people. Music can do four important things for your video: affect the mood of your viewer; create atmosphere and take you on a journey; change your viewer's energy level; and trigger a memory.

It is tempting to allow your personal music preferences to influence what music you use in your video. If you like jazz, you may be swayed to play a piece of music with jazz piano under your opening sequence of shots. If you're a classical buff, the thought of a boppy rock piece might horrify you. But remember that the music in the video has a narrative purpose, and that purpose is audience-centered. Try not to choose music just because you like it; choose it because it will do something for your story. What can music do?

Music Affects Mood

Great composers have used symphonies to tell stories. A classic example is Tchaikovsky's *Romeo and Juliet*. If you listen to it, you'll find it takes you through the moods associated with Shakepeare's classic play. Music can make you feel happy or sad. It can make you feel playful. That is its magic.

However, to affect the mood of your viewer, you need to choose the right music. Getting this right is critical because many people react differently to the same piece of music. You need to know your audience to get this right. Different demographics will respond differently to varied types of music. Sometimes it's about age, while at other times it's about common interests. For example, the baseball song, "Take Me Out to the Ball Game" will not achieve the same effect with a European viewer that it would with an American. And a heavy metal track may not provoke the same response in an older audience as it might with a younger audience. When you couple the right music with video, it can add a powerful emotional message to your story. For example, if you are conveying a serious message, you certainly don't want to have music in the background that belongs at a circus. Likewise, for a lighthearted video, you don't want to feature a funeral march.

Music Creates Atmosphere

Music creates atmosphere and can transport you to somewhere else in the world. The sound of carnival music can draw on your own memory to help bring alive the picture of a carnival. The sounds of a guitar being played can take you to a Spanish restaurant. If you want to create the eerie scene of a London fog, the fog alone can only do so much. Mysterious music can add that extra mystery to your message.

Music Affects Energy

Music profoundly affects your viewer's energy levels—that's why massage centers play new-age guitar music during therapy, and aerobics instructors use music with a strong rhythm and beat. To keep your video interesting, you can selectively play music at certain times to boost the energy level and thus the interest of your viewer. This can be helpful at the beginning and end of the video piece as well as during moments when the narrative lags. For learning video, someone could show a graphic of key learning points while playing positive music in the background to keep their attention.

Music Triggers Memory

Music also has the power to trigger strong memories. Many people remember special moments when they hear a song associated with that event from long ago, such as a song played at a school dance or on a first date. That's why radio stations will often play music that was popular last summer during this year's spring, with the intention to make you feel good—clever.

Of course, it doesn't always have to be so direct. Playing music from another era can evoke powerful memories or even constructs of that era. Music from World War II can help create a 1940s feel, as the muted trumpet of a slow jazz number may help create the atmosphere of prohibition-era Chicago.

Use Music to Influence Your Viewer

When you plan your storyboard and script, ask yourself, What kind of mood do I need to convey? If you are creating a motivational video, you will want that mood to be upbeat and positive, so a piece of music in a major key signature would possibly work.

What atmosphere is appropriate? Is the video a comedy? Do you need music that would more typically be found at a circus? Do you need to create some energy? Have you just finished a fairly complex video and need to summarize the key learning points? If so, perhaps some energetic music under the narrator's voice will work to add some interest. These are the questions that should guide your selection of music, not whether you like the track.

For example, if you want to convey a sense of fear, as a woman in her 20s walks along a dark street without having her say, "It is scary out here," you could play a piece of music with a strong minor tone and a tense rhythm as she walks. If you wanted to change the mood for the same track, you could use an urban techno beat to convey that she is walking home from a happy night out.

Using Music

Music can be used in your video in all sorts of ways. Here are four tips to help you get it right. You will both see and hear how this works in the interactive elements of this book.

Only use music when it achieves your purpose. That is, when you need it to affect mood, atmosphere, or energy. Don't go looking for a place in your video to include your favorite music track. Instead, go looking for a music track that will achieve your narrative purpose.

Strike a careful balance. You should be using music liberally, as it is a powerful tool, but don't overdo it. Some corporate videographers play music underneath the entire duration of their video. All that does is send your viewer into a trance and sets their mind wandering.

Use music for creative repetition. If you're going to recap an important point, a strong, energetic piece of music played behind some commentary or while you are showing a slide is an excellent way to energize your viewer or recapture their attention.

Use music for punctuation. If you have a longer video and need to create separation within it between various chapters, music could be ideal.

Sound Effects

Sound effects are often overlooked by amateur videographers. However, they can amplify your message and make it stick. Sound effects grab the viewer's attention and are often coupled with captions.

Most professional television programs overlay the video with special sound effects to make these sounds cleaner, crisper, and more powerful. Often, these sound effects have been recorded with the microphone close to the source, and they have been processed through special audio filters to make them sound full. When you watch TV, listen to the sounds that accompany the action. For example, there is a sound when someone closes a car door. That sound was likely added in postproduction. The throaty roar of a car as it takes off is almost always more throaty than in real life.

Sound effects are powerful because they draw on both your brain's memory and imagination to make the sound personal. If I were to play the sound of a dentist drill to you, how would you feel? Most people immediately cringe because it triggers that experience in the dentist chair. The sound creates a powerful reaction, because enough bad memories are associated with that sound effect that our brains can imagine and recreate those memories from the starting point of sound.

Every sound has this potential. If you have ever been in a car crash, the sound effects of any car crash will trigger your memory and you'll relive some of the emotions. The visual image is no longer abstract, but is made real by your own memory. Adding sounds to your video will help your viewer experience more of the emotion about the message.

Sounds do a number of things for us. They grab our attention. Some documentary makers will insert a "whoosh" sound at the time a caption comes on the screen. This sound grabs the viewer's attention and encourages us to read the caption.

Using Sound Effects

Think about your message and ask yourself where sound effects can make the message more emotional and powerful. Breaking glass, car crash, slamming door? Replace the original audio from your video with commercially recorded sound effects, which are processed to sound very real.

When you record on a low-end camera, adding commercially recorded sound will give it a real boost. Even on higher grade cameras, you will probably have your microphone focused on your subject, not the sound, so the original sound captured by the camera's microphone will never sound quite as good as when experts do it. Also, if you have a caption or special transition, consider using a sound effect to give it some more oomph. This will draw the viewer's attention and disrupt them if they lost interest or started falling asleep.

Use sound effects subtly, however. The key to using sound effects is to use as few as possible to convey your message. Amateurs tend to overload their media with too many sound effects and draw attention to the sounds, not the story.

Legal Issues With Music and Sound Effects

It is illegal to republish music without permission of the composer, performer, and publisher. So if you think a song by Madonna might suit your video, you must get her and the publisher's permission. If you don't, you are violating copyright and she and you could be sued. It is usually not very convenient to use music performed by popular artists. They often attach stringent conditions on when you can use the music, how it can be used, and even how many times. And they also tend to charge a lot of money for royalties.

Because of this, a whole industry exists to support radio, television, and cinematic producers with music that has fewer strings attached. Known as the production music industry, businesses in this industry compose, perform, and publish music for you to use in your videos. The music is called *royalty free music*. Very often, production houses produce 60-second, 15-second, 8-second, and 4-second versions to give you much flexibility in using their music. It's great for TV and radio stations because their commercials tend to be 60, 30, or 15 seconds. It's also good for you in case you have music that you want in videos of different lengths, and it saves time spent editing the music.

Production music houses offer music in multiple genres. They will offer styles such as orchestral, hip-hop, jazz, rock, easy listening, and even comedy. In the old days, you'd buy a series of CDs or records from this library. Today, you can buy one track at a time by searching their libraries online and downloading what you need.

How much does it cost to use this music? Well, that depends on the publisher and the artist. The music is royalty free, which means you don't have to pay a fee every time you use it. You do need a license, however. Generally you buy a nonexclusive license to that music when you buy the CD or download the track. The license is nonexclusive because anyone else can buy that music track and use it too. Virtually all the music you hear in radio commercials and documentaries come from production libraries.

Many production houses also sell sound effects. You can buy whole CDs of sound effects or download individual sound effects for as little as $3 per effect. Like production music, you need to buy a license to use these sounds. When you buy production music and sound effects, make sure you get the documentation that explains your license and file it away safely in case you need it in the future. Often, video sites like YouTube will contact the creators of videos that have high views and demand to see their license with the threat of taking the videos down. That's why filing discipline is important. Make sure you file your license agreement in a folder you can quickly find when asked to provide proof of your permission to use the music. Every production house will have its own set of rules, and you need to read them to avoid being prosecuted for breach of copyright. Some companies will allow you to use the music only on the web, whereas others will allow you to use it in anything from cinema to radio commercials.

Where do you find production houses selling royalty free music and sound effects? The easy thing is to do a Google search for "royalty free music" or "royalty free sound effects." This will bring up a range of suppliers. You may also find sites offering free music or sound effects. Be wary of these, and make sure you get proper documentation when downloading their audio, because sometimes it can be pirated from other suppliers.

As of printing, here are three companies that offer music and sound effects:

- **Sound Rangers.** This California-based company has a top range of music and sound effects. You can listen to them online, purchase, and download. Many of their effects have been used by Hollywood. (www.soundrangers.com)
- **IB Audio.** This UK-based company offers a subscription. For an annual fee, you have access to their entire library for a year. They offer the best value with the fewest strings attached in their royalty free agreements. (www.ibaudio.com)
- **The Footage Firm.** Based in northern Virginia, the Footage Firm sells royalty free video footage as well as music and sound effects. They charge commercial rates, but don't worry when you first see their prices. They often have specials that give away music and sound effects for the cost of postage and handling. (www.footagefirm.com)

Create Your Own Music

There is the conventional way of getting music for video by buying royalty free content, but you can also create your own music. If you are musically inclined, your first option is to sit down, compose it, and then record yourself or someone else playing it. Perhaps you have a friend or colleague who might do this for you.

Composing music from scratch adds a lot more work into the production process, but it offers you the opportunity to properly craft music to your purpose. If you have the time and resources to do this, that's great. Here is one suggestion if you are recording your own music: Make sure each instrument is carefully miked and that the overall recording is balanced well. This is complex and is both an art and a science.

A new easy way of creating music for your video is making soundtracks with loops. Loops are very short audio recordings of beats or rhythms that last about four bars. You can repeat these and lay other loops over them to create new music. Loops generally sound more electronic than acoustic, but they give you enormous flexibility. If you choose to go down this route, you can easily find loops by searching for them online. You'll find some firms offering loops for free as well as standard commercial sites that sell them. Don't forget, regardless of whether you pay for loops or whether they are free, check that you have the license to use them.

Summary

Music and sound effects can add power to your video and reinforce your message. Adding music allows you to affect the mood and energy level of your viewer, as well as to transport them someplace. Music also has the ability to draw on a positive memory. However, always choose music that is appropriate for your viewer and be careful not to lace your video with music you like rather than what works for the viewer. Sound effects are also powerful tools for giving your picture greater impact. You must have the copyright of any music or sound effect you use. You can buy royalty free production music and sound effects that give you a license to use them in your productions.

Section 3:

Preproduction

So far we looked at the relationship between learning and video in section 1, and then we looked at how video works in section 2. Now in section 3, we start looking at the practical side of putting it all together.

Video production generally follows three stages. These stages are called *preproduction*, *production*, and *postproduction*. Making video involves a lot more than turning up on location with a video camera and shooting some footage, although for many people, that's what video seems to be about. It's not. Much of video production is about planning. If you look at successful television shows, the secret to their success is how they plan their shows. BBC Television Trainer Simon Fox puts it this way: "What takes the time is not filming. It's the planning [by] asking, What shots do I need? Where do I put the camera? How do I compose the shot? And moving from location to location."

Media Coach Jess Todtfeld, who has worked as a producer for NBC, ABC, and Fox, echoes Simon's comments. "Have a schedule so it doesn't last 19 hours for a 30-second video. The part that takes longer [in video production] is the setup. If you can do that before you go on location, then you'll have a smoother, faster time."

In my experience, both in the media and in the corporate worlds, the amount of time required to produce video is always underestimated. I have lost count of how many executives ask for a video to be produced overnight without understanding the amount of time needed to plan. Simon Fox says, "A lot of people who don't make video or television programs grossly underestimate how long it takes and how careful you have to be in planning. It's not just a case of putting the camera down and switching it on."

So as we look at the preproduction process, bear in mind that most of your time will be spent in planning and thinking through your shots, making sure the location is suitable and safe for filming, and creating schedules (so people turn up for the shoot and your crew shoots everything in the most efficient order).

CHAPTER NINE

Preproduction Workflow

In this chapter:

- Preproduction process
- Identify how viewers will learn the learning objective
- Draw a storyboard
- Scout out a location
- Finalize your storyboard and write a script
- Plan the production and logistics
- Plan how to handle and label media assets
- File away your paperwork

Preproduction

Once you have commissioned your video, you go into preproduction. For learning video, this starts with a standard instructional design process that includes identifying a need, establishing a learning objective, and doing a task analysis. You will probably have a general idea of what the video will involve; however, now is the time to get specific and test your ideas to make sure they will work.

Identify How Viewers Will Learn the Learning Objective

You know what your learning objective is. How will you help the viewers learn it? Let's say it is a simple task that every trainer needs to do from time to time, such as connect a data projector to their laptop. You could use a written list, show some diagrams, or shoot a video with commentary to explain the process.

We'll make a video. We need to break down the task into each individual stage just as an instructional designer completes a task analysis. It might look something like this.

1. Assemble a laptop, projector, and VGA cable.
2. Connect VGA cable to laptop.
3. Turn on projector and computer.
4. Adjust computer settings to duplicate monitors using the F4 key.
5. Adjust the keystone function to ensure that the projection is not warped.

Once you have broken down your task, you will then consider how to convey this information. Will you talk about it? Does it make sense to show some video of it? Use some graphics?

Draw a Storyboard

This is where you become creative and draw a storyboard of each sequence you intend to produce. Very often you can draw a storyboard immediately after you have done your task analysis. For more complex shots, you may need to scout your location first. However, for our example above, you probably do not need to scout the location before drawing the storyboard, because it's simple enough. Taking the task analysis, we can plan the visuals that will display each step. As you think about each shot, ask yourself, Does this make this part of the process clear and easy to understand?

Here's a shot sequence for this video. You'll notice that to make it interesting, we decided to contextualize the video by having learners walk into a seminar room.

1. Text Graphic: "Connecting a Data Projector for Your Class."
2. WS of trainer in front of seminar room watching learners walk into room, shot from behind learners as they walk.
3. WS of learners walking into room from trainer's perspective. They sit down and look at the trainer.

4. Text Graphic: You will need your laptop, data projector, and a VGA cable.
5. WS of projector and laptop sitting on desk with cables coiled up next to them.
6. Text Graphic: "Locate the VGA socket on the back of the projector." CU of VGA socket.
7. WS of trainer plugging VGA cable into VGA socket of data projector.
8. Text Graphic: "Connect VGA cable to laptop."
9. CU of VGA socket on laptop computer.
10. WS of trainer plugging VGA cable into socket on computer.
11. Text Graphic: "Now adjust computer to duplicate monitors with F4 key."
12. CU of trainer pressing F4 button.
13. WS of laptop screen showing display options.
14. Text Graphic: "Now set the keystone."
15. CU of menu button on projector.
16. WS of trainer pressing the button.
17. WS of projection on projector screen showing the menu function as trainer toggles down to keystone option.
18. CU of trainer pressing menu function button to adjust keystone.
19. WS of projection showing the changes in the keystone.

Once you have drawn your storyboard and planned the pictures, it's time to find a location.

Scout Your Location

You can never be sure of where to position your camera until you have actually scouted out your location. Without scouting your location ahead of time, it's difficult to plan any contingencies. Sometimes you will need to scout your location before you do the storyboard. For the example above, what if the conference room was an odd shape? You may need to be more creative with your camera because there is less space for wide shots. How about lighting? Is there plenty of natural light? There are other things to take into consideration when you scout the location other than looking at where to position the camera and what shots you can get. Is the lighting sufficient? If you are shooting outside, are there shadows at certain times of the day? How about the noise? If you are conducting an interview in a restaurant, will people be walking by, constantly distracting the viewer? Is there music in the background? Are there safety risks?

Finalize Your Storyboard and Script

If you have drawn a storyboard before scouting your location, you may choose to change parts of your storyboard and script, which is absolutely fine. That's why we scout the location. Having completed your storyboard, add your commentary and put together a script following the two-column format. Include any music or sound effects in your script. When it's finalized, it's time to start planning your production. The first part of your script could look like this:

1. Text Graphic: "You need a computer, laptop, and VGA cable." Hold for five seconds.	**MUSIC:** Play intro music for five seconds as text graphic fades under narrator.
2. WS of projector and computer sitting on a conference table with VGA cable coiled up next to them.	**NARRATOR:** It's easy to connect your laptop to a data projector. You'll need a VGA cable to connect your laptop to the projector.
3. Text Graphic: "Locate VGA socket on projector." Hold until words "VGA socket."	**NARRATOR:** The cable plugs into the VGA socket.
4. CU of VGA socket on the back of the data projector.	**NARRATOR:** Usually this is on the back of the projector.
5. WS of trainer plugging VGA cable into VGA socket of projector.	

Scouting Your Location on the Fly

While it's good practice to scout your location ahead of time to carefully plan each shot before you arrive on scene, it is not always possible. Sometimes facility managers will not give you access until the day of shooting, or sometimes you are asked to shoot footage at the very last minute.

If there's no way you can scout your location ahead of time, make sure you build time into your onsite shooting schedule to walk around and look at the space you are filming for additional cutaways and interesting angles. "If I'm not able to scout the location," TV Trainer Simon Fox says, "I put all the equipment down and just walk around the room deciding what goes where. You often need to move furniture around to get a good shot. Then I get the camera out and frame the shot, before I do any lighting or sound."

Having a visual awareness of your location is essential to finding the very best shot, so make sure you allow time to take it all in at the outset. If you are unable to see the location ahead of time, you can still sketch out a rough storyboard, as it will aid you in looking for certain shots. However, you may not follow it to the letter.

Plan the Production and Logistics

If you fail to plan your production, you will waste lots of time and money. It's tempting to skip some elements of planning and rely on your ability to wing it. More often than not, you'll find yourself correcting mistakes, wasting time on having to decide where to put your camera, and then changing your mind again. What sort of things should you plan?

Make sure everyone you need in the production is available. That includes the person who shoots the video, any person who is in the video, and anyone you need to assist you. Aim to keep your production team small.

Make sure the location you want to use is available. This sounds obvious, but it's easy to forget. Make sure everything you need in the location is available. For example, they're not planning to do maintenance that day and turn the electricity off, are they?

Make sure your equipment is available. We go through the equipment you need in chapter 10. There's a good chance you share your video equipment with colleagues in your office, so make sure no one else intends to use it that day. And make sure someone hasn't booked it the day before, because they may not return the equipment in time for you to use it.

Make sure you have your props. In our example above, it's simply a laptop, projector, and VGA cable, along with the training room. Think also about what your actor will wear—company uniform or something casual? Is there a standard safety gear that people doing a task need to wear?

Conduct a risk assessment. What could go wrong when you are shooting the video? Could someone get burned by lights? Could someone be electrocuted? If you're filming something outside, could someone come by and snatch your camera? If you're near traffic, could you accidentally step into the traffic? Write down the risks and then identify steps you can take to mitigate them.

Make sure you have permission. If you're filming in a public place, you probably need to get a filming license. It's almost certain that if you carry a camera around a convention center, shopping mall, or parking lot, you'll get a tap on the shoulder from security if you haven't first received permission.

Get parking permits. This is more of an issue if you are shooting in a city. The last thing you can afford is to plan a shoot somewhere, then lose an hour of production time because you couldn't find a parking space. It may take 10 minutes to find the right person to reserve the parking space, but that's better than losing an hour of filming.

Get security passes if necessary. You should know who needs to be at the production and thus make sure they get the necessary clearances and permissions to enter the premises. This may include temporary ID passes or simply registering their names with security.

Meet with everyone involved. Run through the script together and make sure everyone has the latest copy they need to work from. Make sure everyone knows where to go for the filming and at what time. Create a production schedule that shows their times and clearly states their responsibilities. Even if your team only has two people, make sure you agree on the responsibilities of each person.

Summary

- Make sure everyone in production is available.
- Make sure the location is available.
- Check that the equipment is available.
- Check that props are available.
- Conduct a risk assessment.
- Get filming permissions.
- Get parking permits.
- Get security passes.
- Hold a team briefing.

Develop a Media Assets Storage Policy

It's easy to head out on location, shoot your video, and then come back to the office with it all tucked nicely on a memory card or Mini DV tape. But what do you do with your media assets? What processes do you follow? It's good to have a system for dealing with your media assets that you can consistently follow as soon as you have created them. Everyone will have a different system that works for them. The key is to follow it consistently and make sure everyone in your team follows the same system. Here are some suggestions.

Designate a media storage device. This could be a server in your office or an external hard drive that you keep to store all your media. It doesn't matter. Just make sure you don't file your assets on your desktop sometimes, in a folder at other times, and then somewhere else another time, where you may not find the content.

Once you have designated where you will keep your media assets, create a folder and subfolders to organize them logically. One folder with 800 video files will not help you find footage in a hurry. You could create folders based on the project or around themes.

Whenever you come back from a shoot, save all your video in the storage device. Be disciplined about this, and don't wait until you need to get the footage before you load it onto the server. Consider your shoot as being incomplete until the video is stored on your video drive in the appropriate folder.

Develop a standard way of naming all your video files. There is no perfect way to do this because every business is different. Some people may like to set up naming conventions based on who shot the video. Other people may like the filename to include the topic, shot number, and date it was shot. It doesn't matter, as long as you get a system that works.

If you are serious about your work, you will use every shooting occasion as an opportunity to build up your library of stock footage. Therefore, as you ingest video footage and rename the files, also add metadata to each file so that in the future you can search it. For example, if you have a shot of the entry to your headquarters, include that in the metadata. Next time you need a shot of the front entrance, you don't need to spend an hour shooting it again; you simply pull out the stock footage.

Create a Production File

When you have planned most of your shoot, you should also create a paper or digital file that contains your storyboard and script, production notes, and legal documents. Your script and storyboard are self-explanatory. Your production notes will include schedules, emails to people asking them to be involved, and any equipment or location bookings you have made. It should also include a risk assessment that members of your team can easily access. Your legal documents will include any licenses for music and sound effects that you will use, along with permissions you have been granted to film from facility management groups.

Having a file sounds straightforward. But when you create a video, you are doing so many things that it is easy to have a pile of papers scattered around your desk, which can get lost. You need everything together so it's easily accessible.

Ahead of the shooting, it may help to explain to everyone each person's responsibilities. In professional film crews, people know what the director, camera operator, sound, grip, and other people do. Web video is less likely to be as complex and needn't follow those protocols. But people involved should know what they're responsible for and, equally, what they're not responsible for.

Summary

Most people think that video production is simply a matter of taking your camera out on location and shooting—this could not be further from the truth. Most of the time spent in the production process is during the preproduction stage, where the video is storyboarded around the video's purpose, the script is written, and the production plan is drawn up. The time spent on shooting the video, known as production, then follows and takes less time than many think. In fact, the better your planning, the less time the production stage takes. Finally, all the video is pulled together and edited in the stage of postproduction. Video takes much longer to produce than many people think; it's a complex and time-consuming process.

Section 4:

Production

The production stage is what most people think of when they visualize video production. It involves setting up the shoot, setting up lighting if you are using lights, and shooting the action. It sometimes involves recording any commentary. Each person involved in production should have a production schedule that shows what shots are planned, who is involved, what props are needed, and what equipment is required. Each person should also have a script or storyboard so they can follow the action. If a large number of people are involved, it helps to have a logistics person on board to project manage the process.

The goal of the production stage is to capture video that can be quickly and efficiently edited. Often in the postproduction stage, the editor will make corrections to the video because the video was poorly shot. This happens if poor lighting was used or if the shot was not framed well. If you have the skills to shoot and are well prepared, you should be able to minimize correction time in postproduction.

CHAPTER TEN

Tools of Video Production

In this chapter:

- Five tools you need to make video on a budget
- Video for under $500—recommended brands of the tools to get you started

---

Equipment for Getting Good Shots

If you're anxious to get started making video, you may have turned to this chapter first.

There's a reason this chapter is buried so deep in the book. When it comes to video, the most important thing you can do is plan a visual story that has impact. Without a well-considered objective and visual narrative that explains and reinforces it, your video will fail even if your camera is fancy and your pictures are well shot.

Of course, this applies to most disciplines. No matter how fine a carpenter you are, if you don't have a well-designed house, the house will almost always look ugly and be dysfunctional. No matter how nice your car, if you don't first map out your journey, there's every chance you'll waste time and not make it to your destination.

This does not negate the importance of buying the right equipment and using it properly. But it underlines the importance of seeing your camera as your tool in conveying information. You do need to learn the discipline of shooting video properly.

In this chapter, we will look at the video equipment you need to shoot video, so your video doesn't look like amateur hour. This book is not about television or cinema production, but is about how you can make video for the web that looks great and doesn't sink your budget. So you will not find recommendations for fancy cameras that offer loads of tricks, because this book is about how to make video affordably with cameras that cost next to nothing.

Your Camera

Here is an example of a video camera.

The first thing you need in order to shoot video is a camera. Buying a camera can be confusing because each camera offers a dizzying array of features. So where do you start? Here are three principles to guide you as you select a video camera, plus the four functions you need on it.

Three Principles for Selecting a Camera

When you look for a camera, buy one that is simple to use. Don't be sucked into all the features that offer red-eye removal, on-board editing, and special features like black-and-white mode. These are things you should add in post-production, not production. Simple cameras are also quicker to use and are less likely to confuse you when you're in the field shooting.

Look for a camera that records your video on a solid state recorder or memory card. There's nothing wrong with good quality tape-based cameras, but they add extra time to your routine, because once you have shot your video, you must then play them into your computer in real time. A 60-minute video will take 60 minutes to load into your computer. With a memory card, it's as simple as transferring a file from a USB stick. If you have a tape-based camera, you will need a FireWire cable to play the video onto your computer.

Another reason to consider a solid state camera that records onto its own internal drive or SD card is that it has fewer moving parts, which means there is less to break, especially if you are rough with the camera.

Make sure your camera has an external microphone socket. Microphones built into cameras almost always guarantee bad sound, because they pick up any noise you make if your hand brushes against the camera. The microphone also has to guess where the sound is coming from. When using an external microphone, you aim it correctly the first time. Using an onboard microphone is a sure sign that you're an amateur. While pictures are what make video, audio can seriously undermine your product.

Cameras tend to have two types of microphone inputs. One is a 3.5mm input, and the other is an XLR. Professional cameras have an XLR input because it is a balanced connector that reduces hum, especially when the microphone cable is long. However, for web video, you will not notice the difference between an XLR or a 3.5mm input. If you do want XLR, you can purchase a camcorder XLR adapter. At time of press, prices start at $140.

Summary

- Choose a simple camera and avoid fancy features.
- Get a camera that records on a hard drive or memory device.
- Ensure that your camera has an external microphone socket.

Four Functions Your Camera Needs

When you've found a camera that is simple to use, you need to make sure it has the following manual functions: focus, exposure, audio, and white balance.

Manual Focus

Many of the cheaper cameras only offer autofocus. With autofocus, the camera focuses the picture for you so that it is clear and sharp, and you as the videographer don't need to do any thinking. However, if you want control of your video, autofocus is not a good option.

If you are shooting a video of a worker standing in front of a machine in a factory, your camera has no idea whether to focus on the machine or on the worker. It has to make a guess. So you may find that the machine ends up in focus and the worker is blurry. Some newer cameras claim they can detect humans from static objects, but why take the chance when manual focusing is quick and easy? When you control the focus, you can ensure that the right object or subject is clear. Also, you can be creative and control the artistic nature of the picture.

Another problem with autofocus occurs when you move your camera. The autofocus isn't always quick enough to know what to change focus on and what not to. Your picture then appears blurry because the important subject goes in and out of focus.

Manual Exposure

Make sure your camera has manual exposure. Cameras don't always detect the subtleties in light and color that your eye does, so leaving the exposure to your camera means you are taking a chance. Another problem with automatic exposure is that if something in the frame moves and some light reflects off that object, this will result in a change in lighting, and your camera will instantly adjust for that moment and then adjust back. This does not look good.

Manual Audio

Your camera should have manual audio control. A lot of cameras offer automatic level control (ALC) or automatic gain control (AGC), which at first makes good sense. The gain control turns the volume up for quieter sounds, such as people who have hushed voices, and it turns the volume down when it hears loud noises.

The problem with AGC is that it constantly monitors the sounds so the volume control goes up and down—there is no consistency. This can cause ear fatigue for your viewers, and when you have silence, such as someone pausing in an interview or taking a breath, it will increase the volume of the background, such as an air conditioner or traffic noise. So look for cameras that allow you to set the microphone with manual audio.

Manual White Balance

Another manual feature you should look for is white balance control. We'll explain white balance in more detail in chapter 12. In a nutshell, white balance allows you to adjust the camera to the color temperature of the location where you are shooting. This is something our eyes do automatically, but a task we must manually do on the camera. Without white balance, your picture can end up with an orange or blue tinge. Some of the cheaper cameras do not give you manual white balance functionality but instead offer you the choice to set the camera for filming indoors or outdoors. While manual control is best, presets are at least better than either automatic white balance or no white balance control.

Tripod

The tripod is one of the easiest tools to help make your video look professional. As BBC TV Trainer Simon Fox says, "The tripod is your friend." If you buy a camera, don't go home without a tripod. When you buy a tripod, make sure it has a spirit level and fluid head. A fluid head enables you to both pan and tilt the camera smoothly.

A standard still photographer's tripod without a fluid head will make your pans and tilts look jerky and uneven. In order to make your pans and tilts look good, your fluid head tripod also needs a spirit level to ensure you set the tripod level. While you can spend up to $1,000 on a good-quality professional tripod, at the time of press, you could pick up a cheap but acceptable model for between $75 and $150.

Here is an example of a fluid head.

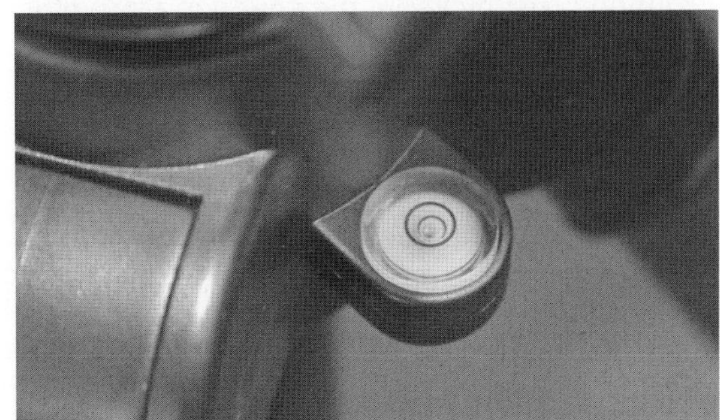

Here is an example of a spirit level.

Microphone

You should aim to have two types of microphones in your video kit. If you can only afford one, buy a shotgun microphone. If you have the budget, also buy a lavalier.

A shotgun microphone, also known as a hypercardioid microphone, is a long cylindrical microphone that picks up the sound in front of it. This means that much of the noise to the side of the microphone is reduced. With a shotgun microphone, you can point it directly at your subject and get a good, clear sound, although the microphone still needs to be as close to your subject as possible without the microphone appearing onscreen. Many shotgun microphones have a feature where you can change the pickup pattern from being sensitive to noise only in front of the microphone to being sensitive to noise both at the front and the side of the microphone. Shotgun microphones can be mounted on the camera, or you can buy a pistolgrip or boom to hold them.

It's worth noting that some of the cheaper shotgun microphones are not always good at limiting noise to the side of your microphone. There are so many to choose from that I recommend you read reviews of each microphone to ensure the model you buy gets the result you want. At time of printing, $200 should get you something decent.

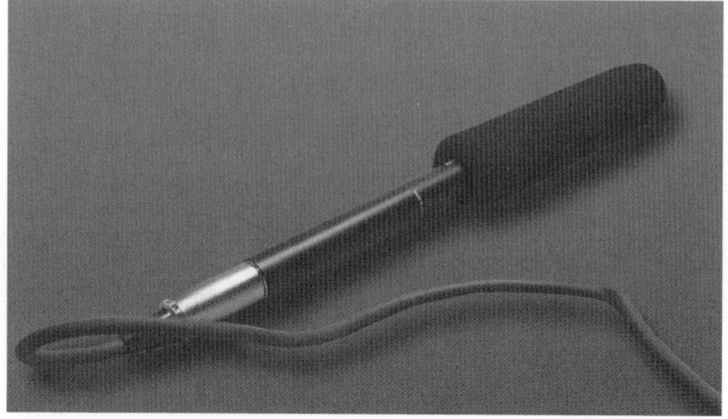

Here is an example of a shotgun microphone.

Here is an example of a lavalier microphone.

On the more expensive side, a lavalier microphone is a small microphone that clips on to your subject's collar or tie. Generally, you will ask your subject to feed the cable inside his shirt so the camera cannot see the cable. A lavalier microphone gets in close to the mouth and tends to focus on the person's voice, cutting out background noise. It's a great option for sit-down interviews, but not good when you are interviewing three or four people in a row, as changing the microphone and rerouting the cable takes time.

When it comes to choosing lavalier microphones, you have the choice between a wired and a wireless microphone. Wired microphones get more criticism than they deserve. They're cheaper than wireless, and unless you're doing lots of walking, you won't trip over the cable. If you want a wireless microphone, however, you will need to choose between a VHF and a UHF model. VHF is prone to lots of interference, but nevertheless is much cheaper than a UHF. You can find a VHF model for about $150, but a decent UHF wireless microphone will cost upwards of $500.

What's best? If you have the budget, go for a UHF True Diversity wireless. A true diversity wireless device operates on two radio frequencies, and a chip inside the unit detects the strongest and clearest signal and sends that to your camera.

Microphones are either a condenser microphone or a dynamic microphone. The difference is that a condenser microphone converts analog sound into electrical current using a capacitor. A dynamic mic uses a magnet. Does it matter? Only to the extent that condenser microphones, which you are most likely to use, require a battery or phantom power. Phantom power is simply power that comes from your camera instead of a battery. Check your camera to see whether it has phantom power. Or better still, always have a spare battery to power your microphones. In practice, condenser microphones can be easier to break, and they don't handle louder sounds as well as dynamic microphones, which are generally more robust and known to withstand a little rough handling.

Editing Software

You need software to edit your video, and once again, you have many options. Back in the old days of film, editors would physically cut the film and then splice it together. It was a simple operation, but a complex art to make sure the cuts were in just the right place to make the action appear natural.

Today, however, editing is done on the computer using nonlinear editing software. You will need to buy an editing program and load it on your computer. The good news is that it doesn't cost very much money.

If you want to do basic editing, Windows Live Movie Maker or Apple's iMovie will work well. Movie Maker is free, and iMovie is available for next to nothing at the Mac App Store. These programs will enable you to cut your video together, add music, and add some special effects, such as titles and credits.

However, if you want to be more sophisticated and add additional graphics and video tracks or manipulate sound and music with more precision, you will need to consider midrange editing programs such as Adobe Premiere, Sony Vegas, and Apple Final Cut Express. You can buy Final Cut Express for between $100 and $150, and the others for less than $100. If you want to get fancy, you may also look at buying plug-ins for your editing software. These range in cost depending on which company you buy them from.

When you are editing your video, you may need to record voice-overs. Simply plug your camera microphone into your computer.

Lights

Even though our focus in this book is on making video cheaply, and thus shooting in natural light, some people may take the extra step and buy lights to improve their images.

We discuss lighting from a broad perspective later on; however, if you plan to add this to your production tool kit, you should look to buy three lights. You will need two hard lights, one soft light, and possibly a fourth soft light if you intend to do four-point lighting.

When you buy lights, you'll be faced with many options and a huge range in price. The good news is that you can pick up lighting kits that cost between $150 and $250, which include all you need for three-point lighting. Some will also come with a green screen should you wish to add chroma-key.

Video for Under $500

Every month a manufacturer will release a new camera, microphone, or software package. And it will promise to do more exciting things and bring a heightened level of technology to the consumer. So searching for the right video camera, microphone, or software package can be stressful.

Here is some equipment that meet the standards we set out already. This will save you the head-scratching work of reading the spec sheets of 20 different cameras and will help you find a camera that will get good results. It is current as of printing. Based on these pieces of equipment, you can build a video production kit for less than $500.

Cameras

Canon VIXIA HF R200 Flash Memory—This camera is the lowest of the VIXIA range and offers the manual features necessary to make great video. It has an audio socket to plug in your external microphone, plus manual control for audio, focus, and exposure. It shoots on a flash card so you can easily transfer video onto your computer.

Sony HDR-CX360V Camcorder—The Sony HDR is closer to a thousand dollars but offers the all-important external microphone. It also offers features such as auto-stabilization, although it has face recognition and other features that we recommend you don't use.

Aiptek Action-HD GVS 1080p HD Camcorder—You can pick up an Aiptek GVS for less than $150. It's very much like a FlipCam except it has that all-important external microphone socket. Price and the microphone socket are two strengths, but it has some negatives such as no manual focus, manual exposure, or manual audio. It does have a limited white balance function. But if you're looking for a cheap starter camera, this is your camera.

Tripods

Here are a few tripods that will get you going and provide excellent support for your camera.

Velbon DV-7000 Video Tripod With 2-Way Fluid Head—This tripod has a fluid head for smooth panning and tilting and can hold a camera of up to 10 pounds.

Velbon VMATE607F Videomate 607 Tripod With PH—368 2-Way Fluid Head—This tripod has a fluid head and can support a camera of up to 15 pounds.

ProVista 6510 Tripod With V10 Fluid Head—If you're lucky, some shops will stock the ProVista with a folding dolly that will give your tripod wheels for those rare occasions when you need a tracking shot.

Microphones

It can be confusing to hunt down the right microphone and be sure the quality is up to snuff. It's a good exercise to do research and read reviews, because you'll learn a lot about microphones, when to use them, and where. However, if time's tight, here are a few quick recommendations.

Nady SGM-12 Shotgun Electret Condenser Microphone. Easy to mount on a camera and can be used as a handheld. This is a super-cheap option and will cost less than $50. This microphone requires an XLRF to mini-phono cable that connects to your camera.

Azden SGM-1X-Super-Cardioid Shotgun Condenser Microphone. This costs less than $150 and will get you a more respectable sound than the Nady. This microphone requires an XLRF to mini-phono cable that connects to your camera.

Shure SM11-CN-Omni-Directional Lavalier Dynamic Microphone. You will need an XLRF cable to connect this to your camera. It will cost around $100.

Sennheiser EW112-p G3 Camera Mount Wireless Microphone System With ME2 Lavalier Microphone. This has a mini-phono plug so it will connect directly into your camera. It costs around $650.

Editing Packages

People argue all day long over the best editing package. Despite what some may say, it is a mixture of subjectivity and looking for what you can get out of it. It also depends on what computer you use. If you spend most of your time in a classroom and want to make quick and cheerful video that looks good but isn't too fancy, you'll best be served by:

- Windows Live Movie Maker if you have a PC. Download it for free.
- iMovie if you have a Mac.

If you want more control to manipulate sound and pictures, or plan to spend a day or more per week editing video, opt for the following:

- Sony Vegas Platinum if you have a PC.
- Adobe Premiere if you are familiar with and like Adobe's Creative Suite products.
- Final Cut Express if you have a Mac.

If you're planning to become a pro and build an in-house production unit, you'll want something along the lines of:

- Avid, Premiere Pro, or Vegas Pro if you have a PC.
- Final Cut Pro X if you have a Mac.

Putting Together Your Camera Kit

You do not have to spend as much money today for equipment that will get you good results as you would have several years ago. But you do need to choose carefully so that you have control over it. At a minimum, you will need a camera, tripod, and external microphone along with editing software for your computer. When you choose a camera, make sure it has an external microphone and manual controls for focus, white balance, exposure, and audio. Avoid buying fancy cameras with tricks like multiple face recognition, onboard editing, and the ability to turn your footage into black and white. Instead, buy good-quality equipment that is simple and uncomplicated.

If you are looking to purchase equipment, you might find yourself in a photographic store or electronic retailer talking to a sales enthusiast whose job it is to sell you a camera that brings in revenue. She may suggest all sorts of accessories, options, and features for your equipment. I know not all stores have sales staff like this, but many do. Don't be intimidated by this because it can be very distracting.

Look for equipment that fulfills the criteria we have covered above and you'll be in good shape. The criteria above offers you the minimum set of equipment that you need to shoot good video and is what professional videographers look for.

The key to buying good equipment is not to be seduced by gear that offers loads of bells and whistles. Go for equipment without fancy functions but that has basic manual controls. Don't be enticed by things like onboard editing, which is not used by any professional I know. (They always edit using a software package.) Don't be enticed by cameras with multiple facial recognition settings that promise to give perfect focus to faces. The professionals I know and have worked with trust their eyes rather than the camera, so paying additional money for such functionality is a waste.

CHAPTER ELEVEN

How to Shoot Great Pictures

In this chapter:

- Choosing the right location
- Using electric lighting
- Aspect ratio
- Framing your shot
- Background noise
- Safety

Tips and Tricks

Why is it that some video looks better than others? For example, when you watch a professional video, the pictures draw you in and focus your attention on their message. How do the professionals make their pictures look so good, when amateur video often lacks the same confidence and visual presence?

In this chapter, we're going to look at how you can make your video look professional and how to avoid the amateur look. We're also going to explore how to use your video to draw in your viewer and ensure that they understand your message. These are professional techniques that will easily work for you on your $300 camera, just as they work on a camera that costs $30,000.

Choosing the Right Location

We've discussed in an earlier chapter how important it is to choose a location that reinforces your story. For example, if you are interviewing a scientist, do it in a laboratory so the picture informs your viewer that your guest is a scientist. If you interview a bus driver, getting him to sit in his seat behind the wheel as he answers your questions will create more interest for the viewer. But there are other things you need to consider in getting the best possible shot. Here are three things to think about: traffic, distractions, and lighting.

Traffic

When you set up your location, check both vehicular and people traffic. Often you will find yourself shooting in public spaces such as a convention center, shopping mall, or by the side of the road. You will have people who normally walk by and through the space you are shooting.

Do you want people in your shot? Will they change the meaning of your shot? Will they dilute your message? If so, plan to have someone redirect the traffic away from the filming location so the people who are irrelevant to your message don't draw attention away from your message. Alternatively, if you do want people walking through the shot, think carefully about where they should walk and have someone ready to direct them to ensure that they don't come into parts of the frame in which you don't want them.

Distractions

When you are filming, it's easy to be so focused on your object that you miss what else is in the picture. This can happen a lot when on location. You will find yourself cropping the video in post-production, which unnecessarily wastes time.

If you're shooting a management training video in someone's office, are there any objects on the desk that are unrelated to the story? Let's say the video is about having telephone conversations and you're using a colleague's office for the shoot. When you look through the camera, what's on the desk? If your colleague's lunch is in view, remove it unless it is relevant to the training video. Likewise, think about what you can include in the shot to boost your story. For example, if you're shooting a video about work-life balance, place a photo on the desk, of the actor's significant other or of the actor walking his dog on the beach, to highlight that there's life outside work.

Lighting

It's critical that your location and in particular the subject or object you are shooting are well lit. Most domestic cameras do not fare well in low-light situations, and your picture will be darker and will lack clarity. You can ensure that your scene is well lit by looking for natural light or by using professional lights. We'll focus more on natural light, although we'll touch briefly on professional lights.

The first thing you need to look for is the main source of light. This is known as the key light. If you are shooting outdoors, your key light is likely to be the sun. If you're shooting indoors, it could be a fluorescent tube that is mounted in the ceiling, or the sunlight shining in through the window.

The key light needs to be directed on the subject or object—it cannot be behind your subject or object where it is directed at the camera. An easy mistake to make is sitting a subject in front of a window for an interview; this creates a silhouette, because the key light is located behind the subject.

Eyes are important in video—both the subject's and the viewer's eyes. Remember that the camera represents the viewer's eyes, so as a general rule, the videographer will focus on a subject's eyes, just as your viewer would look your subject in the eyes if she were listening to him in person. This comes down to where you position your subject in relation to the key light. Some people would think to place them under the office flourescents. But take care.

BBC Television Trainer Simon Fox says that a light located directly above your subject's head, such as the typical fluorescent light found in many office buildings, casts a shadow in the eye sockets and makes the subject look intimidating, because we can't see their eyes. "Don't put people under bright striplights," he says. "Put them slightly to the side."

When choosing locations indoors and relying on natural light, look for bright rooms where the light fills most of the corners. When you shoot outdoors during the day, you will be relying on the natural light of the sun. Here are two tips for getting the best out of your outdoor shoots.

Avoid shooting in the middle of the day. This is when the sun is almost directly overhead and is at its strongest. Because of the angle, it creates a bright, harsh light, which is uncomplimentary to people's skin tone—skin tends to look pale and dry. The best time to shoot is in the afternoon or morning, when the angle of the sun is lower and the light is diffused.

Watch out for clouds. If you shoot on a day with sunny and cloudy periods, your lighting conditions will be constantly changing. Keep an eye out for clouds that pass by and limit the light as well as cast shadows on your location. When you are filming, it is easy to miss these subtle changes.

Extra Step—Using Electric Lights

Because this book is about shooting didactic web video fast and cost-effectively, it is assumed that you intend to shoot in natural light without additional electric lights. However, you may want to take your production one step further and use lights.

Lighting in documentaries is often functional compared to what you find in Hollywood, where lights are critical tools for creating atmosphere and drama. For the didactic videographer, however, you're less interested in creating drama than you are about helping your viewer see the person or activity on the screen.

The basic lighting setup for shooting people in interviews is known as the three-point lighting setup. To understand it, you must understand a few basics about lighting, plus a safety caution.

Safety

There are significant safety issues to consider when it comes to using lights. It's such a serious issue that at the BBC, production staff must pass a test before they're allowed to use them in the field.

First of all, lights get very, very hot. Many people have gotten serious burns by accidentally touching the head of a lamp when it's been turned on for a short while. So when using lights, take extra care to make sure no one touches them, and turn them off so they can cool down before taking them down. Carelessly used lights have been known to start fires and melt plastic objects.

Second, lights involve electricity. Anything involving electricity is a potential safety hazard.

It's even more critical when more than one person is involved. Third, lights have a lot of cables. And cables are easy for people to trip over. Yes, you might say that cables are obvious and adults know how to avoid tripping over cables, but any safety office will tell you that's not the case. Everything needs to be taped down. Clearly mark where cables are, so that people can avoid them.

Lastly, the combination factor comes into play. Any of these issues alone can be problematic. However, if someone trips over a cable and it brings down a light, it could electrocute someone, burn them, or start a fire. If you plan to take advantage of what lights offer, please take care.

Hard and Soft Lighting

Lighting is generally described as being either hard or soft. **Hard lighting** is what you see when you shine a flashlight on an object. It is focused and casts a lot of shadows. The object on which you focus your flashlight is very clear. With hard light, you get to see the object's or subject's texture in great detail. **Soft lighting**, however, casts few shadows and tends to smooth over the texture. Unlike hard lighting, it seems to wrap around objects.

When you are using lights for video, you will have to choose between hard and soft lights. Hard lights often come with barn doors, which are flaps you can use to cover the light or direct it. Soft light comes from using umbrellas, silk, or soft boxes to diffuse the light.

Three-Point Lighting

The standard lighting style used in documentaries is known as three-point lighting, because three different lights are used to light up a subject. The three lights are: key light, fill light, and backlight.

The **key light** is generally a hard light that illuminates one side of your subject's face, although sometimes a soft light can be used. The key light is positioned at a 45-degree angle to your subject and is aimed down at them. Being a hard light, it brings out the texture in your subject's face and creates some shadow around it, so that onscreen, one side of your subject's face is lit. It's important to locate the light so it is aimed down at your subject. That way, the shadow it creates ends up on the floor and the shadow from the nose ends up below the nose, not across your subject's face.

The **fill light** is generally a soft light that is aimed on the other side of your subject and is located at a 45-degree angle toward them. As we discussed earlier, soft light tends to wrap around objects, so it dispels shadows on this other side of the face. The fill ensures that your subject is lit on both sides of the face.

The **backlight** is a hard light that is placed behind your subject and is aimed down at her. It should be high enough up so that it is not in the frame of the shot. This light will draw out the texture of the hair and shoulders, creating an outline that separates your subject from the backdrop.

Four-Point Lighting

Four-point lighting is much the same as three-point lighting, except you aim a fourth soft light on the background. This is important when the background is dark or has shadows. This fourth light is called a **set light**. This is especially helpful when shooting people behind their desk, if they have a bookcase that is lost in shadows.

Cross Lighting

If you have two people in a shot, you may choose to use **cross lighting**. This is where you have two key lights, rather than a key light and a fill light. The key light lights one person, and its beam fills the other person.

Aspect Ratio

Aspect ratio simply refers to the shape of your video screen. It tells us the ratio between the X and Y axes. Traditionally, television was shot in 4:3. However, today most television is shot in 16:9, which is commonly referred to as widescreen. YouTube and most online video sites display their videos in 16:9 widescreen, so do what you can to always shoot in 16:9. Apart from it being the standard for today, it also looks classier.

This shot is displayed as the traditional 4:3 aspect ratio.

This shot is displayed as the widescreen 16:9 aspect ratio.

If you have video that was originally shot in 4:3 but your screen is 16:9, then you can choose how you will display it in a widescreen format. Your choices are:

Stretch it so it spreads to 16:9. This is not a good option because people appear fatter.

This 4:3 shot has been stretched to fit 16:9, which makes the actors appear wider.

Cut the top and bottom of the picture off so the dimensions remain the same, but you lose the top and bottom of the picture.

This 4:3 shot has been cropped to fit into a 16:9 screen. Notice that parts of the top and bottom are now cut off.

Display it on the screen so that there is a black space on both sides of the picture.

This 4:3 shot has been placed into a 16:9 aspect ratio without changing the picture. Now it has black bars on both sides.

Framing Your Shot

Once you have set up your location and determined (hopefully) to shoot in a 16:9 ratio, it's time to frame your shot. We've already discussed the standard shot sizes used in video, but how do we make sure our pictures are more than just a point-and-shoot exercise and instead emphasize our story? Here are three rules followed by filmmakers that will make your web video look much smarter: rule of thirds, looking space, and camera distance.

Rule of Thirds

The rule of thirds divides your picture in three vertical columns and three horizontal rows by imaginary lines. The rule of thirds states that your picture will look better if the object or subject is positioned at a point where the lines intersect.

There are many theories about why this works, and they apply to all visual art, especially photography and painting. One theory suggests that when you position an object or subject on the intersection, it looks asymmetrical and incomplete, which creates a desire in the viewer's brain to see it completed, hence drawing the eye in anticipation. What does it mean in practice?

The actor's eyes are positioned at the intersection of the top and right lines to follow the rule of thirds.

First, don't position your object in the center of the screen.

Positioning the actor in the center of the screen instead of at the intersection of the lines makes it look uninteresting.

It's tempting if you're looking for symmetry, but symmetry is not what we're trying to achieve. Second, when you shoot a person, position their eye on the top line. Don't position their eyes on the bottom line, because then there will be too much **headroom**.

In this shot, there is too much space between the actor's head and the top of the screen. This space is called headroom.

If it's a mid-shot, you'll chop off their hair, but that doesn't matter. Their eyes are what we're looking at. Third, position any object at the point where lines intersect. It could be at the lower left or the upper right.

Looking Space

Have you ever had a conversation with someone who doesn't look you in the eye? It can be disorientating. The same effect happens on-screen when a subject's eyes are looking out of shot. This is impersonal, and we counteract this by creating what's known as **looking space**. When you frame your shot, create space on the screen where your subject is looking. Not only is this more natural, but it also creates a more personal relationship. The same rule applies when panning. If someone is walking, make sure they have space in front of them.

This shot looks natural because the actor has looking space.

This shot looks unnatural because there is no looking space.

Camera Distance

In some shots, it will be important to have the backdrop clearly visible, and in other scenes, it will work better to have the backdrop out of focus. For example, if context is really important, you want your background to stand out. If someone's emotions are more important than context, it may be good for the background to be out of focus.

Let's say you are doing a mid-shot of a subject. You can set this up either by moving your camera closer to the person or by using your zoom control. When you position your camera physically closer to your object, your background will remain sharp.

We can see the background clearly in this shot because the camera is positioned close to the actor and the zoom is set on wide.

The background in this picture is not clear because the camera is positioned away from the actor and the lens is zoomed in on the actor's face.

But if you use your zoom lens to create a close-up, the background will become blurry, while your subject or object remains sharply in focus.

Background Noise

Poor audio can sink a really fine piece of video. So while this chapter is mostly about visual elements, I would be remiss not to discuss some audio issues that occur on location. The three things to look out for when you set up your audio are: public noise, acoustics, and wind and rustling.

Public Noise

Using the right microphone is critical for ensuring you don't get too much background noise in your video. If you're shooting outdoors, this becomes really important, because noise from people talking, sirens, buses, and trucks can drown out your audio or at least distract from it.

Another risk to watch out for is music. If you are in a public place and there is a busker nearby or someone playing canned music over a loudspeaker, it can be distracting. But worse still, if you record an interview with music in the background and want to edit any part of the video, the fact that you cut out part of the footage will be very obvious, because people will notice when the music skips a beat or even worse, skips a whole verse.

When you are shooting, do your best to scout a location that has very little noise. If you want ambiance, such as the sound of people chatting or laughing, record that separately and dub it in later when you get to postproduction. That way you can adjust the level so it is loud enough to be heard, and create the atmosphere you want, but not loud enough to distract.

Acoustics

Acoustics can affect the quality of your audio too. Avoid interviewing people or having people speak in rooms that have a lot of echo. It just does not sound natural and is very difficult to remove in postproduction.

Unfortunately, TV crime shows like *CSI* hoodwink us into thinking that we can separate noise and voices from recordings because they do so in their programs. But the reality is we cannot do this without also damaging the rest of the audio. It's virtually impossible to correct audio in postproduction, so it's super-important to get it right when you first shoot.

When you scout locations, look for rooms that do not have many glass or parallel surfaces, because they are reflective of sound. Rooms with a lot of furniture are excellent at absorbing noise and reducing echo.

Wind and Rustling

Wind that blows in the background can both obscure audio and distract your viewer, so avoid shooting outdoors in areas that have lots of wind. Avoid shooting indoors where you cannot turn off the air-conditioning. These sounds are virtually impossible to remove in postproduction and tend to undermine your audio quality. When shooting outdoors, get a wind sock to place over your microphone; they come in all shapes and sizes. Some are acoustic foam, while others are synthetics that look shaggy and are often referred to as a "dead cat windscreen."

Another thing to look out for comes with using lavalier microphones. When you place one on someone's tie or shirt, you should run the cable under so it is not visible, but make sure the microphone itself does not scrape against any clothes, or else you'll get a soft scraping sound. How do you make sure of this? Once the microphone is attached, ask your subject to move their arms and hands, and listen in your headphones to be sure the microphone isn't rustling against their clothing.

Safety

An often-forgotten element of getting great shots is safety. Why is safety an element of great shots? If your camera is stolen, you're knocked over by a car, or someone is electrocuted by exposed electrical cables, you'll have no picture at all.

Safety starts when you set up to shoot. Watch out for loose cables that may trip people or for exposed electrical wires that may electrocute someone. Make sure people don't go near your lights, if you're using lights, because they are very hot and can burn. Make sure that if you're near traffic or a railing, someone stands with you while you film. When you're looking through a lens, it's easy to forget there's a 10-foot drop behind you.

Before every shoot, conduct a risk assessment. What's a risk assessment? It's where you sit down and write what types of risks you're likely to encounter when shooting your video. You then take each one and write down what you'll do to mitigate that risk. If you're shooting in a team, pass a copy around so everyone is aware of the risks and exercises caution.

Shooting Great Video

Having prepared your storyboard and script and having prepared your production, it's time for you to start shooting video. To capture video that looks professional, take care with your location so there's nothing distracting in the background, and make sure that anything you include, such as background and props, reinforces your story. As you set up each individual shot, frame it by following the rule of thirds and adding looking space to ensure that the picture is engaging and draws in your viewer. Take care with background noise, because even with phenomenally framed shots, poor audio can undermine their strength. And at all times, take into account safety issues and plan to avoid safety risks.

CHAPTER TWELVE

How to Use Your Camera

In this chapter:

- Four steps for getting the best shots
- Shooting for the edit
- Three- and five-shot formulas

Learn Good Habits

Your camera is as important to you as a hammer is to a carpenter. Use it well, and you'll create great video. Use it poorly, and you'll produce unremarkable video. We've talked about how to compose your shots, but how do you ensure that your shots are captured correctly?

In this chapter, we'll go through the four basic steps of setting up your camera. We'll look at techniques that prevent poor-quality video, and we'll discuss a practice known as shooting for the edit.

If you do not use your camera well, you will create more work for yourself down the track when you have to either reshoot footage or spend time in postproduction correcting poorly shot footage. These techniques will help you avoid that. The best way is to make these techniques a habit so you do them without thinking.

Simon Fox describes what was drummed into him by his mentor as he started out in television: "It's just as easy to learn bad habits as it is to learn good habits. So you might as well learn good habits because you always revert to bad habits under stress."

A lot of people in my seminars and at companies where I consult and coach tell me they know how to set up a camera and shoot good video. But when I see them in action, they break many of the rules. Their shots are wobbly or poorly lit, or the audio sounds awful. I can't emphasize enough how important it is to get into the habit of doing everything properly. It may seem like a lot of work at first, but you'll find it becomes automatic. Plus, your shots will be better than many other people's.

Setting Up Your Camera

Before you do anything, you need to set up your camera. That involves assembling it and mounting it on a tripod. If there's one thing that dramatically improves video professionalism among amateurs, it is using a tripod.

You'll need to set up your tripod properly. Make sure that it is level by adjusting the legs and using the spirit level. Then, screw the quick release mounting plate onto the underside of your camera and lock the quick release plate—which is attached to your camera—onto the tripod head. Set the camera angle, and tighten the locks so the tripod head doesn't droop forward and tilt down. If you have any cables, tape them down so no one trips over them. This includes power, microphone, and lighting cables.

As a general rule, it's good to always charge the battery of your camera and run from battery power. Sometimes when it's plugged into an outlet, the camera picks up an electrical buzz from the outlet. Also, if you're in the middle of filming and the power goes out, your battery will keep things going. It will not always be possible to run on batteries, but if you can, do so. Plus, it's one less cable to trip over.

Four-Step Camera Setup

Once you have set up your camera on the tripod, there are four things you need to do. We're going to run through the general principles because using these functions and finding them in the menu will be different for every camera. When you shoot, remember these four tasks: white, light, tight, and bright.

White (White Balance)

The first thing you need to do is set the **white balance** of your camera. The color white, such as a white sheet of paper, looks different under different types of light. If you put it in the sunshine, the white will look slightly blue. If you place it indoors under typical light bulbs, it will look slightly yellow. As well as white objects having these different shades depending on whether you are indoors or outdoors, every color in your shot looks as if it has been tinted with that cast.

This is not a problem for the naked eye, because humans can detect this and adjust. Our cameras can't, so we must make the adjustment for them. Some cameras do this automatically. Other cameras offer presets in the menu options such as, "film under sunlight" or "film under tungsten."

To be sure your white balance is set properly, you should do it manually. To white-balance your camera, go to your white balance controls in your camera's menu and select manual white balance. Hold a sheet of white paper in front of the lens and zoom in so nothing but the white sheet of paper is in view. Then click the white balance button. It will spend a few moments comparing the sheet of white paper to its own presets of whites and adjusting each color in proportion.

What happens if you don't set the white balance? Depending on where you shoot, your picture may appear yellow or blue. Always set the white balance whenever you move to a new location.

Light

When you have set your white balance, you should set the exposure according to the **lighting**. Once again, you will find the controls for exposure in your camera's menu. Looking through the viewfinder or at the screen, adjust the light so that it is light enough to see everything but dark enough not to lose detail.

When the picture is overexposed, you have too much light and will lose subtle details; a wrinkle on a white shirt disappears. Overexposed shots cannot be rescued in postproduction.

When your picture is underexposed, it will not have enough light, will look lifeless, and once again you will lose detail. If you underexpose your picture, it will be easier to rescue, because there is at least some detail to play with.

Tight

The next step is to properly focus your camera. Remember, autofocus is not a good option. **Focusing** means adjusting the lens until the picture is sharp. If you're shooting the edge of a knife, it should look crisp and clear. The key to focusing correctly is to zoom in on your subject or object and then focus. Even if you will not use a close-up in your video, you can zoom back out to set up your shot size. Whenever you move the position of your camera, refocus.

Some cameras have a focus assist button. If you press it, it will magnify the picture so you get an even larger picture, which makes it easier to ensure that the focus is absolutely crisp. Once you have your shot in focus, zoom back to whatever shot size you had intended. Your picture will look sharp now, regardless of how close or how far away you zoom.

Bright

The final thing to check is that your sound is **bright** and clear. There are two things you need to do to check your sound: first, check the audio levels on the camera; second, listen to it on your headphones. Your camera should have a manual audio function in the menu. Select this and you will see a digital display that tells you how loud your audio is. The display is a series of bars that shows the sound levels. Zero db is the loudest, and it can go down to anything as low as –90db.

You can adjust your sound level manually. More expensive cameras allow you to do this with a dial on the side of your camera, whereas less expensive cameras tend to give you this control with a multifunction toggle or touch screen function. When you have found the audio settings in your camera's menu structure and selected manual audio, ask your subject to speak at normal volume and adjust the volume until it registers around –20db for speech. Any loud noise will be higher than this, but aim for it to be no louder than –10 db. This will ensure good sound levels.

As you adjust your levels, listen to the subject's voice in your headphones. Is she close enough to the microphone? If she isn't, the room may create an echo sound. Does she sound clear? Perhaps the microphone is too close and she sounds muffled. How about the microphone placement? Can you hear rustling because the microphone is placed near a flap on her clothing? Change the microphone position by moving it closer to or farther from her mouth, and adjust your audio levels on the camera until her voice sounds bright and clear.

If you have the resources, you may have access to different types of microphones. If you have a sit-down interview and it is one person, opt for a lavalier microphone. If you have several people, a shotgun mic will make it easier to redirect the microphone to the person speaking as each person takes a turn. If your subject is walking and talking at the same time, a wireless mic would be ideal.

Shooting for the Edit

Once you have shot your video, you need to cut all the shots together so they can make a sequence. There are two things that often make the editing process longer than it needs to be: poor-quality shots and lack of additional shots for cutaways.

Poor-Quality Shots

When your shots are poor quality, you will need to spend time correcting them. The sorts of things you may find yourself fixing up in the editing process include exposure, white balance, focus, and even image stabilization. This takes time and is a waste, when correctly shooting the video the first time would require no more effort later. Often, making the necessary adjustments during production will add one or two minutes to filming. Making the adjustments in postproduction will add five to 10 minutes as you correct various levels of contrast and brightness, and additional hours when the video is rendered.

Another problem editors often face is that part of the action is cut off. This happens when the videographer presses start on the video camera at exactly the same moment the action starts, because the camera doesn't start capturing the action until a few seconds after the start button has been pressed. Starting after the action gives the editor very little breathing space to cut into the shot.

While shooting videos seems straightforward and is in fact simple at times, getting good shots is complex and requires your brain to do many things at the same time. Yes, it is easy to make mistakes. However, with practice, good techniques will become automatic.

Some people don't spend the time to learn these techniques. They often think that they will easily fix any problems in the editing process. Almost always, fixing problems while editing takes more time than when you learn to do them correctly in the first place. I don't want to sound like an autocratic schoolteacher. Rather, I want to encourage you to save time by getting great shots at the outset. The time spent editing should not be spent fixing problems. It should be spent enhancing an already top-notch video. That might include using chroma-key, converting to monochrome, or adding other special effects.

Lack of Necessary Shots

Earlier, we compared a video sequence to a sentence and video shots to the words that make up a sentence. The camera operator's job is to go fetch the words for the sentence or, in video terminology, get the shots. The editor's job is to construct the sentence or, in video terms, make the sequence, by placing the pictures in an order that makes sense to the viewer.

Very often, the editor finds herself sitting at her computer trying to create a sequence without enough shots to convey the message. Without the necessary shots, the editor has to become creative and find other ways of conveying a message that the missing shot should be conveying. Sometimes she will create special effects, and at other times she will manipulate existing shots to compensate for the missing shot.

If you have planned your video by starting with a storyboard, you should not find yourself in this position. However, in the stress of shooting video fast, it's easy to forget to capture additional B-roll shots to make the sequence more visually interesting. So we need to develop techniques when shooting that can prevent issues like these from causing problems during editing, which makes the process longer.

Speeding Up the Editing Process

What can we do as we shoot our footage that will speed up the editing process? You can: draw a storyboard; roll your tape early; remember not to cross the line; shoot additional cutaways; and use shot formulas.

Draw a Storyboard

Back in chapter 5, we talked about how important it is to start with a storyboard. One of the reasons a storyboard is helpful is that it disciplines your mind to think carefully about the pictures you intend to shoot. The second reason a storyboard is helpful is that it forces you to look at each individual shot, and ensures that you plan every shot you need to convey your message.

Therefore, if you have a storyboard and you follow it when you shoot, then you most likely will capture every shot you need for your sequence. This will save lots of time in the edit. A storyboard also ensures that we are clear about what we need to shoot, which saves time having to think up shots on the run. It also saves us shooting more footage than we need, because we only shoot what we want and then spend less time sifting through useless video that we ultimately discard.

Roll Your Tape Early

To make your video footage easier to edit, start recording 10 seconds before the action starts. It's very easy to press start on your video camera just as the action starts. However, there is usually a lag between when you press start and when the camera starts recording. So if you start recording only when the action starts, you will miss the first second of that action. This makes it very difficult to edit. Therefore, when you shoot, press start on your camera and then wait 10 seconds before calling for action. Likewise, wait 10 seconds until after the action has finished before you press stop on your camera. This is a good habit to get into because this extra time gives your editor more to play with when cutting all the shots together.

Don't Cross the Line

In chapter 5, we talked about the 180-degree rule. This rule suggests that we look at the floor plan of the area we are shooting, divide it in half with an imaginary straight line, and then shoot from only one side of the line. The 180-degree rule ensures that our view is not confused when we cut from one shot to another shot. If we cross the line, it will disorient our view and make editing much more difficult.

Shoot Additional Cutaways

We have discussed the importance of regularly changing your shots for the viewer. Most likely, you will have planned enough shots in your storyboard to achieve this. However, when you are shooting on location, it is likely that you will see other possible shots that did not occur to you when you were planning and may add to your story. You might discover certain visual possibilities that did not exist when you scouted the location and that will also add to the story. After you have shot the shots planned in your storyboard, shoot other shots that you notice. You may not need to use them all while editing, but they are a great backup should you need them.

My experience is that when you work with a professional videographer, she will often point out visual elements at your location that will really add to your video. Shooting these in addition to the shots you have in your storyboard gives you more to play around with in the edit.

Shot Formulas

It is important that you draw the storyboard before heading out on location to shoot your video. However, you may find yourself in a situation of having to produce a video with very little notice. How do you ensure that you can create enough shots to make a visually compelling sequence?

There are two techniques that you can follow. One is known as the three-shot formula. The second is known as the five-shot formula. If you follow these formulas when shooting, you will shoot enough footage to create a compelling sequence in the edit. The key to these shot formulas is to shoot your action a number of different times. Each time you shoot the action, use a different shot size or camera angle. This means that when you are editing, you will have multiple shots to choose from in order to create interest.

Unlike multi-camera work, where you can shoot an action once and get many camera angles and shot sizes with different cameras, single-camera work requires you to redo the action several times. If you are showing somebody walking in a park, you would shoot that sequence three or five different times, using three or five different shots, and using many positions, angles, and shot sizes. You then have three or five different shots of the same sequence to create variety in the final edit.

The Three-Shot Formula

You use the three-shot formula when you shoot the action three times from three different positions using three different shot sizes. Generally, you'll go for the following three shots:

- wide shot
- close-up
- mid-shot.

Let's say we are shooting a video of a woman walking down a path in a public park and sitting on a concrete block. If we use the three-shot formula, we shoot the action three times as follows:

1. WS of park with woman walking.
2. CU on woman's face as she walks.
3. MS of her sitting down on concrete block.

If we had only shot this as a single wide shot, it would be a boring 15 to 20 seconds. But by cutting between these different shots, the sequence becomes visually interesting.

The Five-Shot Formula

The five-shot formula follows the same principle, only with five shots. These extra shots give the editor more visual content to play with to make it more interesting to the viewer. If you follow the five-shot formula, you get the following five shots:

- wide shot
- extreme close-up
- close-up
- mid-shot
- additional angle, preferably a creative shot.

Let's consider the same action from the perspective of the five-shot formula. It could look something like this:

1. WS of woman walking on path.
2. CU of shoes on pavement.
3. CU of woman's eyes.
4. BIRD'S-EYE of woman sitting down on concrete block.
5. MS of woman resting head in her hands.

The five-shot formula ensures that we have plenty of different pictures of the same action. This way, we can make the sequence more visually interesting.

General Rules for Three-Shot and Five-Shot Sequences

When you are editing between shots, it's important to make it look as natural as possible. Part of this requires you to achieve continuity when you shoot the footage. This is necessary whenever you do more than one take of an action. Make sure that when you repeat each shot, you repeat it exactly the same way each time. For example, imagine you are shooting a video of a woman in her office and she reaches for her cell phone to type a text message. You may be cutting between a mid-shot and a close-up. Let's say you cut between the mid-shot and the close-up as she lifts her right hand over the phone to type the message. It would look awkward if she lifted her left hand in the mid-shot and her right hand in the close-up when you cut between the mid-shot and the close-up. Not only does this look unnatural and fake, but it also makes your video lose credibility.

Summary

The production stage is likely to take less time than preproduction and postproduction. However, using your camera correctly will have a big influence on how much time you need to spend in postproduction. Spend the small amount of extra time required to get your shots correctly, and you'll save much more time in the editing suite. That means manual white balance, exposure, focus, and audio. (White, light, tight, and bright.) Make sure you have a storyboard to save time in shooting and to prevent wasted time in the editing suite having to discard useless footage. Make sure you get the extra shots you need by planning for them and looking for them after you have shot your video. And pay attention to continuity and adopt the practice of rolling your camera 10 seconds before action.

CHAPTER THIRTEEN

Looking Good in Video

In this chapter:

- How to help people feel comfortable when appearing in your video
- How your subjects should dress to look good in your video
- Grooming tips
- Tips for looking great

Making Your Subjects Feel Comfortable

We've spent most of our time talking about how to make good video. But the people who will appear in your video will worry less about how to make good video and more about how they can look good onscreen. In this chapter, we're going to look at a few things you can do to help the subjects in your video look great.

Your role as a videographer is to make your subjects look good onscreen. In didactic video, you are generally interviewing people or featuring them in your video to focus the viewer's interest about a certain topic.

Therefore, the better they look, the less you distract the viewer from what they are talking about. One of the first things that will distract your viewer is your subject's emotions. Simon Fox says, "Usually when people are at ease, they will be a lot more natural. And it's very unnatural to be in front of a camera with a blinking red light." He suggests talking to them beforehand. "I explain to them what I am doing. If someone has never had a mic attached to them, it can be a scary feeling."

If your subject is nervous or uncomfortable, it will immediately show, so you need to make them feel comfortable on camera. This is not always easy. Most people are not used to having a box with a lens pointed at them. There are a number of things you should do with your guests to make them more comfortable and to ease their nerves.

First, make sure they know what you want them to do. If they're going to talk about a subject, be very clear about how it will fit into your video or the overall series of videos that you are shooting. Explain to them what you are expecting from them. Give them an overview of how the production process works. Tell them you will need to set up your camera, interview them, shoot some cutaways, and, if it's an interview, shoot some over-the-shoulder shots of you asking questions.

Make sure you don't just explain this to them when you first ask them to be in the video. As you work with them, explain what you're doing each step of the way. If you're changing your camera position halfway through, tell them you need to keep the shots interesting. You don't want them thinking that all of a sudden you thought they looked bad from that position.

As you shoot, listen to their thoughts and questions. Being on camera can be nerve-racking for many people. If they need to tell you they are nervous, let them tell you, because you'll find it calms their nerves. In fact, the more they feel they are having a natural conversation with you through this process, the more relaxed they will be. Of course, you will be mindful of your deadline and be sure to keep the show going. Just remember that you need to attend to their needs to ensure that they are comfortable. I find that the more they focus on me asking them questions, and the more we have eye contact, the more relaxed they are and tend to forget the camera is there.

If you are interviewing someone, never give them your questions ahead of time. It's OK to tell them the areas you would like them to discuss, but never give them your exact questions. The reason for this is twofold: First, if you agree to the questions, you will be held to a rigid script and they will complain if you deviate. Frankly, good interviewers almost always leave their scripts; they shape the interview as the interviewee makes her comments. This is what makes a dynamic interview.

Second, when guests know the questions ahead of time, they often rehearse the answers, which always turns out wooden and unnatural during the interview. You don't want them reciting an answer they memorized and practiced in front of their bathroom mirror—you want them to have a natural conversational tone that suggests spontaneity and draws in your viewer.

Another tip about interviewee management relates to how you manage your relationship with the person. You should never promise you'll use the interview. If it turns out your subject matter expert is awful onscreen, adds nothing interesting to your topic, or just goes off track, you don't want to be held to it. You also need to have the freedom to use three minutes of their comments or just 20 seconds. So never give guarantees and instead tell them their interview is one of a number of important interviews.

How Your Subjects Should Dress

If there's ever a topic to get you in trouble, it's talking to someone about how they dress. This is one of those conversations that can be deeply personal and can lead to all sorts of arguments. One of the problems with how many people dress is that they choose clothes that they like the look of. They see them in a magazine, on a department store mannequin, or on someone who they think looks hot. This is not the way to choose clothes. The secret is to choose clothes that look good on the person, not on a mannequin or someone else.

Now this is not always easy, because they will turn up for the shoot wearing what they think looks good, when very often it is something that looks good on other people. If you have control over what people wear in your video, the first step is to help them be aware of their body shape. Yes, this can be a sensitive conversation, so take it easy. We could ignore this, but how many training videos have you shown to classes where the participants spent time laughing at how actors were dressed, what their hairstyle was, or about the width of their tie?

The first principle to remember is that it's a fallacy that some people look good in anything. The reason people look consistently well-dressed is that they consistently wear clothing that works for their body shape.

For example, I look lousy when I wear pants that have a high-rise waist. That's because the average pair of pants that has a waist of 34 inches tends to look baggy on anyone under five-foot-nine. I'm five-foot-eight and a half. Therefore, if I want to look professional, I need to look for short-rise pants. If I had more weight around my waist, I would also avoid pleats, because they exacerbate wider waists, and opt instead for flat-front pants, which tend to make you look skinnier.

The problem is that like many people, I have to fight the temptation to buy clothes I like over the need to buy clothes that look good on me. This is not a book on fashion, so rather than categorize every body type, it's best for you to talk to a style consultant or buy a book that helps you identify your body type and choose clothes that look good on you.

In addition to thinking about body shape, think also about fashion. The key here is to avoid fashionable clothes and encourage people in your videos to wear classic fashion.

10 Tips for Dressing Well on Video

Here are 10 tips that are specific to looking good on video. You may find this to be very personal, but that's the nature of video. Video is all about how people look and the impressions they create.

1. If someone does not have a strong jawline or has a double chin, get them to wear a V-neck and avoid a crew neck top.

2. If someone is rotund, get them to wear darker colors around the thicker parts of their body and lighter colors around their slimmer parts. Darks reduce the appearance of weight. While I tend to recommend avoiding stripes, vertical stripes can make someone look slimmer, while horizontal stripes make them look fatter.

3. If your subject is tall and skinny, ask them to wear different tones for the upper and lower body, as this will even things out. Likewise, if you want someone to look taller, suggest they wear the same color, as it will create a longer eye-line.

4. Avoid showing off lots of skin. When you have a subject matter expert on camera, you want your viewer to be watching her eyes as she talks. Plunging necklines and bare shoulders can

distract the viewer. Unless you're on location at a gym, tank tops aren't a great idea. Likewise, hairy arms are distracting too—men should opt for a long-sleeve shirt. By the way, when women have plunging necklines or exposed shoulders, they often create a visible contrast on video between their faces, which have makeup, and their shoulders that don't. Cameras pick up these details that we easily forget.

5. Avoid wearing garish or loud jewelry. I'm not suggesting no jewelry, but think about how it looks and sounds. Dangly earrings can be distracting, bracelets can make a sound when bumped against a desk, and shirt cuffs can make noises when banged against a desk. While we're talking about garish, men should never wear ties with Daffy Duck or pictures of their kids on them. It's distracting and looks unprofessional.

6. While we're talking about ties, learn to tie a Windsor knot, which looks good, and make sure your tie reaches your waist or belt buckle. A lot of men still tie their ties so they only reach as far as their belly button. Not only does this make them look like a school kid, it also makes them look fatter. Likewise, don't let them appear on camera with a half-tied tie—not if they are a subject matter expert.

7. Avoid bad fabric and glaring colors. That means polyester blouses, shirts, and ties. These reflect light and are distracting. Also avoid the color white. "The camera is not very good with the color white," Simon Fox says. "You tend to get a horrible shimmery effect and very bad contrast. If you look at television medical dramas, you'll see the lab coats are actually off-white. As are white walls. This is known as television white."

8. Avoid stripes and herringbone. These can create a strobing effect in video.

9. Make sure your clothes fit. If you buy an off-the-shelf shirt, it may not be designed for your dimensions. It is designed for the average person's dimensions who, by the way, doesn't exist. Often the sleeve is too long and the shirt billows out in the back like a tent. Get the shirt altered because longer sleeves bunch up around the shoulders and make your subject look

disheveled, while short sleeves look awkward because they make you uncomfortable. People often wear ill-fitted coats. If the coat is too big, he looks like a kid dressing up in his dad's work clothes. If the coat is too tight, he looks awkward.

10. Make sure your clothes are not crumpled. That means iron them or have them dry-cleaned. Crumpled clothes make people look disorganized and out of control.

Grooming Tips

There are a number of grooming tasks that can make someone appear better onscreen. The first is to get a haircut. Long hair looks unruly, and you want to look your best. It's a good idea to encourage your subjects to have their hair styled several days before you interview them so it has a chance to settle into place.

My second tip is for men. Shave before you go on camera rather than when you leave in the morning. If you're shooting your subject after lunch and they shaved before they came into work, they will start developing that five o'clock shadow. It is especially noticeable with men who have dark hair. You want your subjects to look fresh, not tired.

If you can give your subject enough warning, they may want to try some teeth whitening. All I'm suggesting is the whitening strips you can get from the local drugstore. Smiling with shiny white teeth beats smiling with stained yellow teeth.

If your subject wears glasses and you are using lights, the lenses are likely to send off a distracting reflection. If possible, ask your guest to appear without glasses. If you have enough time to give them notice, suggest that they ask their local eyeglass shop for nonreflective coating of their glasses.

My last tip for grooming is makeup. Most women are comfortable with foundation and compact powder. Many men, however, find the thought of wearing makeup terrifying. But one of the little problems that occurs when shooting men on video is reflection on the area above their nose and across their forehead. If you're shooting with lights, this is especially problematic. Before you go on camera, use some foundation to even out your skin tone, then add compact powder on the shiny parts of your head above the nose to avoid reflection.

Tips for Looking Great on Camera

There are many tips that seasoned television professionals could offer that will help your subjects look better on camera. Here are just a few of my thoughts.

1. Make sure your subject has a comfortable but straight posture. It's easy for them to slouch, especially if you're spending more than a few minutes shooting. Make sure they have a straight back, but not so straight that it looks uncomfortable.

2. Seat your subject at a very slight angle to the camera—about five degrees—so she has to turn ever so slightly toward the camera. Facing the camera head-on looks two-dimensional and flat.

3. If your subject is standing, have them stand more at an angle to the camera, perhaps 40 to 50 degrees, as it will make your subject appear slimmer and is more appealing.

4. If your subject has a double chin, get them to lean toward the camera, as this will minimize it onscreen. Leaning toward the camera will also make you appear slimmer. New York–based Media Coach Jess Todtfeld explains it best. "Whatever is closest to your camera is going to appear the largest on your screen. So if you're sitting back in your chair and your head is farthest away, your stomach will look bigger and your head smaller." He suggests sitting on the edge of your seat and tilting your pelvis by 15 degrees. "Tilting 15 degrees forward feels a little strange," Todtfeld says, "but it looks awesome and amazing on camera." Use an object to relax your subject. Some people look really awkward in front of a camera when they stand. I will often get them to sit on a stool at a slight angle to the camera and then move their head to face the camera. Or I'll give them something relevant to their topic to hold in one of their hands.

Learn From the Pros

These few tips are a great start to help you think about the things you might do to make your subjects look better onscreen—but a list like this is no substitute for a well-trained eye. Over time, you'll add to these and possibly modify them to work for you.

The best way to evolve your expertise here is to watch how the pros set up their interviews on television. Look at how the subjects perform and what mannerisms they display. Also look at what sort of things distract you from their eyes as they speak.

Many of the television techniques carry over to web video. However, you'll probably spend more time doing mid-shots and close-ups for web video because your subjects will be watched on a computer screen or mobile device.

Section 5:

Postproduction

Postproduction is where you make sure the raw video footage looks good, cut it together, and then add any special effects. Editing is a very complex process and requires real skill to make the pictures cut together without looking awkward.

The first thing that happens in postproduction is that the video is logged. If it's been shot on a camera with a memory card, the footage is saved into the video files. Once it's been saved, the file names will be renamed to suit your naming convention. If the video was shot on tape, the tape will need to be digitized or played into the computer. It is then saved in the appropriate folders. Then the editing and addition of special effects begins.

CHAPTER FOURTEEN

Editing Your Video

In this chapter:

- Art of editing
- How to save time in postproduction
- How video software packages work
- Choosing a video editor

Editing Words vs. Video

The concept of video editing is similar in some ways to editing the written word. And just as it is important to put words in the right order to create coherent and powerful sentences, putting shots together in the right order is crucial to creating powerful sequences. And as editors of the spoken word look for a natural flow in the way words work together to create meaning, video editors look for a natural flow in the way pictures cut together to create meaning.

The main difference between editing video and the spoken word is that you'll use video editing software. And because you're manipulating pictures rather than text, it will be slower, because video software is manipulating video files (which are larger). Your computer requires more processing power for larger files.

While no two video software packages are the same, there are many similarities. The basic entry-level video editing software packages come free with your computer, or at least for next to nothing. Windows Live Movie Maker and Apple iMovie enable you to bolt together your pictures by way of a virtual storyboard. You simply import your shots and then drag and drop them in the order you want to see them. Once they're in order, you trim them so they flow together nicely.

More sophisticated editing packages give you a timeline, which offers greater precision. You position your shots along the timeline and edit down to individual frames or seconds. This precision becomes necessary when you look to create fancy edits, add special effects, and perform complex audio manipulation.

Probably the most common topic of conversation when it comes to editing video is the question of what software to use. We'll discuss that later, because more important than the tool itself is the skill to use that tool. Just as editing the written word is both an art and a skill, so is editing video.

The Art of Editing

Good editors do more than take your shots and position them on the timeline. They use the shots to create a continued sense or flow of time and space within your story. Put another way, editors arrange the shots to make the viewer feel that the event follows a logical and natural progression.

This principle, which is referred to as continuity editing, is important for factual video and gives us a set of rules to follow when using video to construct learning. And while these rules are sometimes challenged and broken in artistic cinema and entertainment, they are important in didactic video, which is less about creative expression and is more driven by purpose.

Steps an Editor Takes

So what steps does an editor take when cutting together a sequence? In the postproduction stage, you should have the video from your camera, your script and storyboard, and some of the graphics you plan to insert into your video. To pull it all together, you'll generally follow these five steps:

1. Ingest the video.
2. Assemble the shots in order on the virtual storyboard or timeline (including graphics such as text graphics).
3. Trim each individual shot.
4. Add cutaways.
5. Add transitions and effects.

Ingest and Log the Video

The first thing you need to do as an editor is get the video out of your camera and onto your computer so you can edit it. This process has different names depending on who you talk to. It's known as *ingesting*, *importing*, and *digitizing*. The process of ingesting your video will be different depending on whether you have shot your film on a tape or on a camera that uses a memory card.

If you have a tape camera, you will need to connect your camera to the computer via a FireWire or USB. Once you have plugged your camera into the computer via the FireWire, your editing software will ask you to identify the camera and accept the connection. Most software packages will allow you to control the play, stop, and fast forward functions in your editing program. From here, you will be able to control the process of playing your video into the computer.

Not all cameras or software packages are the same. You'll need to look at the instruction manual on your editing software for specific instructions on how these controls look on the screen and how to use them, because each program has its own way of ingesting video. You will also need to check your camera's instruction manual, because some cameras may require special software to connect to computers and import files. And of course there will also be variances depending on whether you use a PC or a Mac.

As the software package imports your video, it will recognize shot changes, designate each different shot as a separate file, and assign file names.

When you import video from tape, the ingestion process takes place in real time, and you can watch the video as the computer digitizes it. This can be frustrating if you're in a hurry—however, this gives you a good opportunity to review all your footage as it is played in and to jot down information about your shots that may be helpful to remember later.

As tape cameras become more and more obsolete, cameras with built-in or detachable memory are making the job much easier. If your camera has memory, you'll simply connect your camera and import the video file as if you were importing a file from a memory stick. Each individual shot—that is, the video you recorded between pressing start and stop on your camcorder—will automatically be given a file name.

Preventing Headaches Later

If you want to save time during the editing process, there are a number of efficient housekeeping practices you can follow. Here's a recap:

Create a folder structure that makes it easy to find your video footage and other files associated with a project. Once you start making video of a reasonable length, you'll find yourself juggling multiple files for audio, video, data, and graphics.

Depending on the complexity of your project, you may find yourself managing a hundred or more files. It makes sense to keep them orderly so it's easy to find later without the headache of having to watch every single video.

A project folder structure will help you do this. At first, it will seem cumbersome, but don't worry. Once you have done this a few times, it will become second nature. Start by creating a folder for your project and then adding these sub-folders:

Project—This is where you save your project file. You may have different versions of the same project: one for the IT department, one for the HR department, and so forth. Keep the different project files here.

Footage—Store the video footage that you intend to use in the project in this folder. This includes the video you shot on your camera, plus any other video, such as library footage, that you intend to use.

Graphics—Store your still graphics here. If you have text graphics, still pictures, diagrams, graphs, special logos, or pictures you intend to use, keep them here.

Audio—Store any music, sound effects, or remastered audio you intend to use in this folder.

Finals—This folder is where you keep your final masters. No sense getting them mixed up with all the other files.

Rename each file as you ingest it so that it follows a standard convention. Renaming all your files may seem cumbersome when you can't wait to dive into the editing process. However, if you don't do it right away, the number of files that have not been renamed will grow, and your folder will become an unruly mess. You'll never know where to find key shots, and this will both frustrate and slow you down.

Fixing poorly shot video is time-consuming and unnecessary if you follow the rules for shooting that we covered in chapter 12. However, mistakes do happen, and it's good to know what tools you have to get you out of a pickle. If you do need extensive correction, you can probably save time in the future by reviewing your shooting technique. The one tip for video correction is to do it first, before putting your video into the video editing program. Get into a routine of fixing all the shots and saving them as remastered files that can then be imported with the rest of your video.

Assemble the Shots in Order

Once all your video material has been loaded into the relevant folders, you should create a new project file in your video editor and import your video files into the project. You then assemble the footage in sequence along the timeline in your editing package. You can do this by simply following your storyboard. You will also add in any animation or still graphics.

Assembling your shots is like creating the first draft of a manuscript—you're not worrying about spelling or grammar. With video, you're not worrying about trimming your pictures yet; you're just concentrating on the logical flow. Watch the order and ask yourself if it works. If it doesn't, swap around some pictures and try something new. You don't have to follow the storyboard exactly.

As you assemble the footage, don't worry yet about making the shots look smooth together when the video will play for an audience. At this stage, your shots and any graphics simply need to be in the right place and in the right order. You may need to cut some shots in half and move them around—that's fine. You might also call this the blocking stage because you're putting the blocks together.

Trim Each Individual Shot

Once everything has been assembled in the order you want, then it's time to trim each shot so that it flows naturally. This is part of continuity editing. Believe it or not, many things can disrupt the continuity, and it's at this stage of the editing that the editor's skill is tested. Probably the most important thing to avoid in film editing is creating a jump cut.

Jump Cuts

When you watch television, you'll notice that the shot will change every six to 10 seconds. If someone is walking through a door, the shot change occurs in the middle of the action. If the editor is good, you will hardly notice the change; this is what you want to aim for when editing. However, to make it look natural, you need to avoid what's known as a jump cut.

A **jump cut** is a transition between two shots when the second shot is out of natural flow with the preceding shot. Let's say your actor is lifting his left hand out of his pocket to turn the door handle. Shot #1 is a wide shot taken from behind him, and shot #2 is a mid-shot from the side as he reaches out to twist the handle. In these shots, the actor takes his hand out of his left pocket, lifts his left hand to the door handle, twists it, and opens the door.

With this small sequence, we are going to cut from shot #1 to shot #2 as the actor lifts his hand out of his pocket to twist the door handle. How do we know when to cut? We need to cut between the shots so it looks like the action is continuous.

If we trim the first shot so it ends when the actor pulls his hand out of his pocket, and then trim the second shot so it starts when his hand touches the door handle, it will look unnatural because we are missing the action of his arm swinging up from his pocket to the door handle. This is called a jump cut. It looks jerky, feels awkward, and does not look natural. To avoid the jump cut, we need to trim the first shot so it ends at exactly the same point that we start the second shot—perhaps at the point when his hand leaves his pocket.

Trimming is an art and takes time and practice. Good editors do this in such a way that you will hardly notice the cut. As you edit your video, you may find your shots give you little choice but to have a jump cut. Maybe the video wasn't rolling 10 seconds before the action, so your video starts halfway through the action of him twisting the handle. There are ways to hide a jump cut: one is a cutaway, and another way is to change your shot sizes.

Continuity

This problem is tough to fix in the editing process. Your actor may open the door with his left hand in one shot and then open it with his right hand in the second shot. All of a sudden, the viewer's brain notices that something is off. Alternatively, he may have his hand in his pocket in one shot, yet have his hand hanging beside his leg in another shot.

There is not a lot you can do to fix this in post-production. It is something that you need to think carefully about when you shoot your footage, and convey to the actors. To even use these conflicting shots, you have to resort to all sorts of trickery.

Cutaways

One of the time-tested tools for avoiding jump cuts and for condensing time in video is the cutaway. Cutaway as a term is more prevalent in Europe, while most people in the United States refer to it as B-roll.

A cutaway is a shot that the editor puts in the sequence to hide a jump cut. Usually, this shot is secondary footage the camera operator shot while on location as a backup. (Remember we discussed the importance of getting additional shots while shooting, so you have extra shots on standby for just this purpose.) The secondary footage is known in the United States as B-roll because in the old analog edit suites, you had two rolls of video tape: the main action on A-roll and the cutaways on the second tape referred to as B-roll.

Here are three places a cutaway can save your hide and ensure natural continuity:

- when the footage you have makes it impossible to avoid a jump cut
- avoiding a jump cut when editing an interview
- condensing time.

If we had a jump cut in the top sequence, and happened to have a shot of a sign on the door that says "Joe Smith," we could insert that between shot one and shot two and no one would notice the jump cut. But that's not the only time we may use a jump cut.

Let's say we're editing an interview with a subject matter expert. Halfway into her interview she digresses on a topic that is not relevant to the interview. Unlike audio, if we chop that segment out, it will be obvious, because you'll see it's a jump cut. If we have a cutaway, we can hide the edit and make it look more natural.

The final place a cutaway helps you achieve smooth flow is by condensing time. Let's say your action involves an actor walking down a hallway to the rest room. This may take 15 seconds and makes really boring video. You only need to see the actor walking along the hallway for a few seconds and then briefly opening the restroom door to know he is heading to the bathroom. But if you cut 10 seconds out of the middle, you'll get a jump cut. To avoid this, you can show the actor taking the first few steps, then cut away to another shot, such as a close-up on his feet, and then cut back to him opening the door to the restroom.

Add Transitions and Effects

Once you have assembled your footage and trimmed each shot (or added a cutaway) so that it flows smoothly, it's time to add your special effects and transitions. Editing programs offer you all sorts of special effects. You can slow down a video so it displays in slow motion, transform it into black and white, add effects that make it look like an old TV show, and even adjust the brightness of your shots.

Check your software package to learn about what effects and transitions are available to you. Also, don't forget to research third-party special effects providers like NewBlueFX to see what effects plug-ins you can add to the package you already have.

You may be asking, Why add special effects and transitions at the end of the editing process? In reality you will find yourself making some corrections and adding some effects earlier in the process. But as much as possible, work first on the bones of the video: that is, putting the pictures in a logical sequence; trimming each shot so you don't have a jump cut; and adding any necessary cutaways. It's like building a house—put your frames up first, then add the drywall and paint it. Likewise with video, add your special effects and transitions at the end, as this will speed up production and ensure that your video has a good foundation.

The Art of Editing

Editing video is an art. You don't just throw it all together and hope for the best. At the outset, you plan your video and shoot the action so that everything works well during the edit. And in the edit, you put it all together so that your video has a seamless flow, and your viewer is totally focused on your learning objective—not your edits.

The key for didactic video is to always ensure that your viewer is not distracted by your editing and that your editing is invisible. What do we mean by invisible? We want people to notice your message, not how you cut your shots together. To do this, follow the basic rules we have discussed, and your video will look professional.

It's worth noting, however, that some highly acclaimed cinematographers and television producers deliberately flaunt these rules for effect. For example, a TV director may deliberately use a jump cut to create the feeling of awkwardness. This is fine for entertainment and art, but we're talking about learning video. More often than not, breaking these rules will be inappropriate and will undermine the professionalism of your content.

Video Correction

Another task of the video editor is to correct poorly shot video. Following the steps above assumes that your footage was perfectly shot—but talk to any video editor, and you'll discover that they often have to fix mistakes made by the camera operator.

In Movie Maker, you can brighten or darken your video if it has been shot without adjusting the camera for lighting. That's about as far as things go—however, if you're using Final Cut, Premiere, or Vegas, you will have a lot more control over your picture. It's worth spending some time looking at what each package offers, because they're not all the same.

How Editing Software Packages Work

We talked about the art of editing first, rather than the software itself, because your software is secondary to your ability to craft video attractive to the eye. Once you understand the craft of editing, you should be able to learn any editing software package and get good results. Give a first-rate editor Windows Movie Maker instead of Final Cut Pro X, and they'll still make your video look first-rate.

Software packages come in all shapes and sizes. Most today are nonlinear software systems, which give editors so much more power than they had with traditional tape systems.

Your Original Video File Is Safe

The first thing to know about nonlinear editing systems is that they do not actually manipulate the video you saved in your project file—the original video file is not altered in any way. When you work with a software package, it displays a low-quality version of your video in the preview window. During the editing process, you tell the program you want to trim the shot so it starts three seconds in from the beginning, and you want to trim the end at 9.5 seconds before cutting to the next shot, which starts three seconds in.

While you are doing this, it seems your video editor is changing and joining your video according to your instruction. But it isn't doing anything of the sort—it is simply recording the data of which shot you are using, what order the shots are in, and when you start and finish the shot, along with any special effects, transitions, or audio. This is why project files usually have a very small file size: They're simply data about which video files are being used, where to find them, and how to present them.

When you watch your edited video on the preview screen, it is following the instructions contained in the data file and simply putting together a version for you on the spot, without changing any original files. The playback is often jerky and pauses from time to time because your computer has to catch up with all the information as it goes hunting for the original file, then displays it following the instructions in the data file. This is intensive for your computer's processor.

When you have finished doing your edit, you then select an option in your program to render a full-quality version. You will find this action described differently in each program. Some programs use the term *publish*, others *render*, while others simply *export*. Movie Maker calls it "save movie." During the export process, you tell it the resolution you'd like the final video to be and it takes your instructions for each shot, piece of audio, and special effect, and creates a brand new copy that you cannot change.

A simple way to think of this process is that it is like creating a workbook in Microsoft Word.

You have a bunch of text and graphics, plus a layout style. When you have finished putting your workbook together, rather than send a Word document for printing, you create a PDF, which preserves the exact layout and presents all the individual images and text as one single file. Then you send it off for printing.

Storyboard vs. Timeline

Video editing packages allow you to position your shots together so they make sense. They either follow a storyboard or a timeline approach. Cheaper entry-level editing packages tend to follow a storyboard approach; more expensive programs offer a timeline.

With a storyboard editor, you import the video shots into the storyboard window on your screen and position the shots so they are in the correct order. You can move the shots (they are thumbnails) around so they are in any order you like. This is what a nonlinear editor is all about—it doesn't matter what order they are currently in. Once they are in position, you will trim each shot so they run together smoothly.

Storyboard editors are great for creating video fast. This is how both Windows Live Movie Maker and Apple's iMovie work. They are ideal for trainers who need to create good video fast and don't want to spend time in finicky postproduction. The limited special effects are easy to apply through a simple drag-and-drop function.

Timeline editors have you place the video on the timeline. When you look at a storyboard editor, the thumbnails of your shots do not show whether the shot is 10 seconds or 10 minutes long. With a timeline editor, you can see the picture displayed in terms of its length. While it does not display the video file as a thumbnail, you should see a snapshot of a part of that piece of footage.

Timeline editors provide multiple tracks for you to add each video message layer: pictures, visual effects, graphics, music, spoken word, and sound effects. For more sophisticated productions you can add additional tracks, so that you may have three different tracks for the picture layer, three for spoken word, and so forth. Each track will have its own set of controls. For example, audio tracks will give you control over functions that include graphic equalization, compression, and panning. The graphic equalizer allows you to boost or reduce individual audio frequencies. In some ways, it's just a more sophisticated version of the bass, treble, and middle controls found on many home stereos. The compressor adjusts how loud your audio signal is and has the effect of making your audio sound fatter and fuller. The pan control sets where you want that track to sound in terms of stereo separation: for example, whether you want the track to come out of the left or right speaker.

The video tracks give you control over cropping and over any effects that you add, such as brightness/contrast, chroma-key, or picture sharpening. If you want to create sophisticated video, you will use a video editing program that is based around the timeline and has multiple tracks, allowing you to edit with precision down to a split second.

Choosing a Video Editor

There are many different editing programs to choose from. Which one is best for you? Whenever enthusiasts get together, they start telling each other that the editing software they are using is better than every other software package available. It's not that much different from people who argue for and against Macs and PCs. Generally, it will not be your software that sinks your video—it will be your editing skills. So does the program really matter?

You need to find an editing program that suits your work style. Is the majority of your time going to be devoted to creating video for trainers? Or are you a trainer who spends most of her time in the classroom, but wants to capture interviews with subject matter experts to show participants in her courses? If you're a trainer who plans to create video from time to time—maybe one or two days a month—you'll be best served by Movie Maker or iMovie, because they are easy to learn and do everything you will need them to do. Movie Maker is also free, and iMovie comes bundled with new Macs.

If you expect to spend more than one day a week shooting and editing video, you should consider a higher end timeline-based editor such as Adobe Premiere, Sony Vegas, or Final Cut Pro. You'll be influenced by whether you use a Mac or PC (Final Cut is only available on the Mac). It's important to emphasize that all of these packages are great options—no one is better than the other. It will come down to personal preference.

At the end of the day, your editing software is important. But just as a good word processor doesn't make a good writer, your editing software does not guarantee great video. The full potential of the software you choose will only ever be realized if matched with good video editing skills.

When you choose a video editor, ask these questions in order to make the right choice.

Does it work with the same video format as your camera? If your camera outputs QuickTime files and your editor can't handle QuickTime, you'll need a format converter, which will slow things down. Find an editor that does QuickTime, or get a QuickTime plug-in.

Does your computer have the right specs? Your computer needs good memory and a fast processor to handle high-definition video.

And can the software work in high definition? You should be shooting in high definition even if you output at a lower quality. (As a general principle, always shoot at the highest quality before down converting it, because it will improve your picture. Also, high-definition originals are good for archives.)

Is it easy and intuitive to use? Take a trial version for a test drive. If you already use Adobe products, you may find Premiere quicker to pick up than Vegas.

How much is it? The cheaper the better. Different packages go on sale at different times.

Export the Master Copy

Once you have completed your video, it's time to export it as a final product, which we call the master copy. As mentioned earlier, exporting your master copy is in some ways like exporting a word processor document as a PDF. Just as the images and layout from your Word document are fixed in a PDF document, the cuts, effects, and transitions you apply will be fixed in your exported video. And just as PDF documents tend to be a smaller file size than the original, your master video will likely be compressed and will also be smaller than the original video footage.

Exporting your final video takes a long time because the computer has to do a lot of work. It is at this time that the computer and program are completing the actions you suggested in your editing process. Where the project file says to cut from one shot to another at a particular time, the editing software will render this, along with any other commands you have, such as effects and transitions.

People often get confused about how to export their master copy because they face a lot of options, especially in the more sophisticated editing programs. What resolution? What file format? This is one of those variables that you will need to discuss with your technical advisor or IT administrator. If you are uploading it to YouTube or Google Video, and you are using Movie Maker, there are automatic presets you can select, and this takes the guesswork out. Programs such as Premiere, Vegas, and Final Cut offer presets too, but they are less straightforward.

As technology evolves, the potential of video quality will continue to improve. And as more people consume video content, the demands for higher specifications will increase. Rather than prescribe the best specifications here, it's best to follow the guidelines and standards of the sites on which you will be publishing, for example, YouTube or Vimeo. If you are publishing on an intranet, check with your IT department.

The web video sharing site Vimeo offers information about settings for your video if you are uploading it to Vimeo. It also offers guides on how to prepare the export settings on 28 different software programs. You can look at these at http://vimeo.com/help/compression.

For information on the best settings for loading videos on YouTube, visit http://www.google.com/support/youtube/bin/answer.py?answer=132460.

If you plan to host your video on your company's intranet, you need to consider a range of factors, such as the bandwidth of the average user's internet connection, what software they will be using to watch your video, and the platform they will be watching the video on. For example, will they watch at their desk on their PC, or on the road with a smartphone or tablet? (We talk about hosting later on.) You need to determine the right settings with your technical advisor or IT administrator.

Generally speaking, you should export a high-resolution master copy for your records, and then create a copy at the resolution your technical advisor recommends for posting on your intranet or website.

Summary

It is in postproduction that you will see your video come together. If you have shot good-quality footage and extra B-roll, the editing process will be less time-consuming than if you have to correct lighting or other problems.

The key to editing your video is to be disciplined in how you manage the files and the order in which you complete the tasks. Leave the special effects to last and make sure you block the video and trim it first, making sure there are no jump cuts and that it flows naturally. Remember, good editing is about the craft and not the software. When you look for software to edit video, choose a program that best suits your needs. If you're only making video every once in a while, settle for Movie Maker or iMovie because they're easy to learn. For more complex video, look to higher end packages like Vegas, Premiere, or Final Cut.

Section 6:

Into Action

There is one final production issue to consider as you take your production knowledge and put it into action: workflow. Video always takes longer to produce than people expect. It is complex to plan and produce, and invariably things go wrong, whether at the location or when you edit. Production requires a disciplined approach to avoid doubling or even tripling the time spent making video. Trainers in today's world—whether they are in a corporation or work as contractors—already struggle under a growing pile of responsibilities and deliverables and cannot afford to waste time. So making video fast is critical.

In this section, we touch on the technical issues you need to know about to be a good videographer and to have constructive conversations with your technical team. We also look at how to avoid common mistakes amateurs make in production, and provide a disciplined workflow.

CHAPTER FIFTEEN

Tech Stuff

In this chapter:

- How video works
- Video on the Internet
- Bandwidth and file size
- Shooting to reduce file size
- Video file formats
- Where to post your video
- Making your video available to download
- Streaming your video on demand
- Posting your video onto a video sharing site
- Hosting your video on a commercial video platform
- Publishing your video as DVDs

Understand the Basics

Have you ever sat in a meeting with technical folks when they start tossing out terms like codec, file format, mpeg standard, and compression? As you sit there thinking, "I thought we were here to discuss putting video on the intranet," you do everything to control your body language to look confident and hope no one asks you a question.

Well, don't be alarmed. You don't need to be a technical whiz to create video. However, you should understand some basics. Every discipline requires some basic technical knowledge. And while the knowledge of how to use pictures to tell your stories is more important than knowing the actual bandwidth of your company's IT network, some basic knowledge of how video works as a technology will be enormously helpful.

This chapter is not a technical manual. Amazon is full of great books that delve into far more technical depth than you'll ever need. This simply gives you enough background to understand some of the conversations you'll hear about using video, plus open up some of the reasoning behind what we talk about elsewhere in this book.

How Video Works

The best way to understand how video works is to think of a film strip. A film strip is a series of still images that changes slightly over time. In fact, for every second of action you see on a film, there are 24 individual images that change very slightly. Flipping through 24 of these frames—each of which is slightly different—in the space of a second creates the illusion that the picture is moving. In the film world, we call each individual image a frame.

Frame Rate

The number of frames used per second to create the illusion of movement is known as the frame rate and is measured as frames per second, or fps for short. When you buy a camera, you will see a list of the different frame rates you can set it at. Some people consider having 24fps on their camera a plus, because it looks more cinematic than televisual.

Not everyone shoots at 24fps. While it is standard for cinematographers, U.S. television camera operators shoot at a frame rate of 29.97fps, while European camera operators shoot at 25fps. This is because Europe follows a different television system than America. Frame rates vary on the web.

Television video looks different than cinema. One reason is the frame rate. However, the difference in how the picture is transmitted is more significant. This is explained by understanding the difference between progressive and interlaced video.

Progressive and Interlaced Video

Film strips are what we call progressive. That means that every 24th of a second, you see a totally new image before it progresses to the next frame. However, television technology is not so straightforward—it is based on a system of interlaced lines. Broadcasters transmit the picture as a series of lines with pixels. These lines are easy to see on traditional television sets made from cathode-ray tubes (CRT).

Traditionally, television stations use interlaced video and only transmit every second line of the picture at any one time. That way, there is less information to broadcast at once. They then follow it a split-second later with the alternate lines. This happens so fast that it creates the illusion that the whole picture has been transmitted at once. In the U.S., where video is generally shot at 30fps, 60 half-complete frames are actually broadcast every second.

Why do we need to know this? Good cameras offer the option to shoot in either progressive or interlaced mode, although a great deal of consumer cameras automatically shoot in interlaced. If you are shooting for traditional television or standard-definition DVD, interlaced is a great choice. However, web video is progressive, so you should shoot in the progressive format if you have the option. If you shoot in interlaced format, the edge of shapes in your video will have jagged endings. In this case, you need to go through a process known as deinterlacing. Many editing packages offer this option.

Video on the Internet

Video on the Internet is displayed differently than both film and analog television. Internet video is really just digital data. When you download a video from YouTube, you are not downloading a video, you are downloading digital code that needs special software to decode it and display it as a video. This software could be Windows Media Player, RealPlayer, or Adobe Flash Player.

To put this into perspective, everything in your computer is digital data. What you write in a text document is saved on your hard drive as digital code, not as a document of text. When you open it in a software program, the program decodes the digital data and turns it into text. This happens with images, too.

Not all types of files are equal when it comes to size—text usually requires very little data to record information. But images, audio, and video are made up of much more data. You can see how large image files are when you surf the web. On a webpage, you'll notice that the text downloads faster than pictures. You'll usually see the text immediately but have to wait a few seconds for the images to appear, because pictures require more data than text and take longer to download. The reason for this delay comes down to competition between bandwidth and file size.

The Trade-Off Between Bandwidth and File Size

Bandwidth is the measurement of how fast data can travel along a connection. It's measured in terms of how many bits of data can travel across the connection between you and the Internet per second. Bandwidth is often categorized as either narrowband or broadband. Narrowband simply means narrow bandwidth and broadband means wide bandwidth.

There's no sense putting an actual figure on what constitutes broadband because the figure continues to evolve. When I led workshops about the Internet to broadcasters in Britain in 1999, a bandwidth of 512 kilobits per second was considered broadband. Today, 10 megabits (10,000 kilobits) per second is considered broadband. Next week it may be 20 megabits—all we know is that the capacity will continue to increase.

Bandwidth will affect how easily your viewers access your video. If they have broadband, they should be able to watch video. If not, your video will not download in real time, and may stop and start as they watch it. Because of the restrictions of bandwidth, we are not able to download true high-quality video. Most of it is highly compressed so that the file requires less data.

Bandwidth is a huge issue facing corporations because their connections to the Internet are almost always shared among purposes. And given that video is generally large in file size, you need more bandwidth. If you're in a retail organization and want to make learning video available to all of your stores, you will be competing for bandwidth at each retail location with connections to banks and credit card merchant services. If you're in an office environment, you'll be competing for bandwidth with other workers who are sending holiday photos and email jokes.

File size creates big problems for video on the web. If you have 25 frames per second, then for every 10 seconds of video, you are downloading the equivalent of 250 images—that's a lot of data. There's not a lot you can do about bandwidth, especially if you're sharing your Internet connection with a whole office. But you can take one step to reduce file size, and that's known as compression.

Compression

Basically, our aim is to reduce the amount of data required to display a video. The less data we use, the smaller the file size. The process of compression achieves this by doing two things: First, it will adjust pixels in the picture, and second, it will compress movement. Let's quickly consider both in nontechnical terms.

Adjusting the Pixels

Every individual frame is made up of many square dots called pixels. In high-quality images, each pixel may have a different color value. Often your image will have minor variants in color that are largely unrecognizable to the naked eye. By averaging these out, you can reduce the amount of data needed. The key here, of course, is to only change the differences that are unlikely to be noticed by the eye.

Compressing Movement

The second way to compress video is to record only the changes that take place between frames. Consider, for example, a video of a baseball player running to home plate.

The only thing that changes in this image is where the baseball player is—the green grass and red dirt around home plate remain the same. Instead of recording four or five different frames, we can record a reference frame and then only the data that actually changes in relation to the reference frame.

When we compress video, these are the two things we are doing. Depending on the settings we use when we export our video, we can emphasize one more than the other. The key is to only compress the video as much as we need in order to reduce file size and still maintain quality.

There are two times when you will compress video. The first is when you export the master copy from your video editing software. You will be offered a range of options, and you need to discuss these with your IT administrator. The second time to compress video is after, when you have the option to take a high-quality video and run it through a file format conversion program, such as Format Factory. It will offer you options for the rate of compression, which will often be described in terms of the bandwidth on which you want your video to easily display.

Future of Video

This all seems complex to a new videographer, and it sounds like you have to compromise on quality when streaming video over the web. If you're worried, don't be—the good news is that bandwidth continues to grow. This is due to new technology, including fiber-optic cable, which can carry incredible amounts of data per second.

If you consider the quality of video today compared to 10 years ago, you will have seen video evolve from blurry, smudged images that were the size of a postage stamp into remarkably clear video that can fill up your entire screen. It will only get better. But in the meantime, we need to compress our videos. Besides file size compression on the computer, there are a number of things you can do when shooting your video that will help to keep file sizes small.

Shooting Techniques to Help Compression

To make our video files smaller, we need to reduce the amount of data required to encode the video. However, certain shots will always be difficult to compress, and if we are able to avoid these when shooting, we'll aid the compression process. The more data that changes in the shot, the more difficult compression is, so here are some shooting tips that will reduce the amount of data. In the process, they will also make your video look more professional.

Avoid Moving Backgrounds

If you are shooting an interview and there is lots of movement in the background, your video will require more data, because it needs to create more reference frames. Choose backdrops that have little movement. There are editorial reasons for choosing some backgrounds that have lots of movement—you need to balance these against the need to reduce the file size.

For example, if I want an establishing shot that tells my viewer the video has been taken in London, I might shoot a wide shot of a double-decker bus driving down Oxford Street in London. But that will create a lot of movement and almost everything in my shot will change from frame to frame. Alternatively, a wide shot of Big Ben will require less data because very little will change, except perhaps a cloud in the sky. This shot will still achieve my editorial purpose of establishing the fact that we are in London.

Shoot on a Tripod

If you shoot with a handheld camera, there is very little chance that your shot will not wobble. Every time your camera moves up or down or side to side, everything changes from frame to frame. The same is true for the baseball player shot I described earlier, because the position of the grass and diamond will change every time you move your camera. The only way to avoid shaky shots is to put your camera on a tripod or something that ensures that the camera will not move. If you can't find a tripod, use a monopod, or place a beanbag on a wall or something solid and position your camera on the beanbag.

Don't Pan, Track, or Tilt

Whenever you pan, track, or tilt your camera, every detail in your shot will change frame to frame. This makes compression very difficult and will not help the compression process to reduce your file size. Excessive panning, tracking, and tilting tends to scream out the message that you're an amateur, but compression gives you another good reason to avoid these camera movements.

Don't Zoom In and Out While Rolling

The same principles apply to zooming into or out of a shot while the tape is rolling. Once again, it means your computer will have to use each individual frame and will be unable to reduce data by creating a reference frame and then recording only what changes. And as we also discussed, excessive use of zooming comes right out of the amateur's tool kit.

File Formats

When you see a file that has the extension .doc or .docx, it's recognizable as a Microsoft Word file. There are many word processor file formats: for example, .txt means it's a plain text document and .rtf means it is a rich text file.

Video also has many different file formats too. These have been developed by multiple software companies and camera manufacturers. Some have been developed more for capturing video and are used by your camera, while others are more for sharing. Here are the most common:

- .wmv—Windows (PC)
- .mov—Quicktime (Apple)

- .rm—Real Media (PC)
- .flv—Flash (PC & Apple)
- .mp4—MPG (Motion Picture Group)
- .avi—Windows (PC)
- HDV—Sony (High definition of mini dv)
- AVCHD—Sony and Panasonic

Windows Media Video

Windows Media Player is based on .wmv files. This is a compressed format that you can export video as. It does not naturally work on Macs, and so if using a Mac, convert .wmv files to Quicktime or get a media player for the Mac that plays .wmv files, like VLC player or Flip4Mac. If your trainees have PCs and you are sending them video files, .wmv is a good option for your master video.

Quicktime

Quicktime is the Mac's video format. If you're playing .mov files on Windows, you'll need to get Quicktime for the PC or get a free VLC player. If you're creating video for trainees who will watch the video on a Mac, you should export them as a .mov file. For PC video editors, you will need to download Quicktime.

Real Media

Real Media is a proprietary multimedia format from RealNetworks that is less common than Windows media files and Quicktime. It used to be very popular in the early days of the Internet before Windows took its market share. RealNetworks have the RealPlayer, which is a cross-platform media player that plays .mpeg, .mov, and .wmv files.

Flash Video

Flash video is probably the most popular video-sharing format today. Many news sites, such as the BBC, use Flash to play video because the file sizes tend to be compact, and most computers have Flash installed in their browsers. Most free video sites like YouTube will convert your original video file to an .flv file so that just about anyone can view it.

MPEG and MP4

MPEG stands for the Motion Picture Encoder Group, which was set up to develop digital compression standards, first for television and now the web. .Mpg has a number of stages starting at .mp1 and ranging to .mp7. .Mp2 is the most common; however, .mp4 is increasingly popular and compresses videos into tight sizes.

AVI

AVI stands for Audio Video Interleave and is one of the most popular uncompressed video formats for standard definition. It was developed by Microsoft. While it is popular and offers good quality, the file size is very high and not suitable for streaming. It tends to be compatible with most editing packages.

HDV

HDV is a compressed high-definition format of video developed for lightweight prosumer cameras. It is a tape format that was used in cameras such as the HVR Z1, which was popular with news gathering and documentary producing organizations like the BBC and Discovery before tapeless cameras became popular.

AVCHD

AVCHD stands for Advanced Video Codec High Definition and was developed by Sony and Panasonic. It is increasingly common for solid state cameras that do not use tape, and it uses the .mpg4 codec.

When Will You Use These Formats?

If you're wondering when you'll use each of these formats, there's no certain answer, and technology will continue to evolve, making it something to regularly review. Your choice will depend on the camera you are using and where you'll be displaying your video. For example, some cheaper cameras like the Aiptek will output video as a .mov file. Other cameras will output the video as AVCHD.

If you are streaming video on your own internal e-learning site, you may need to output your final video as Flash. If you're creating video that will be displayed on sites such as YouTube or Vimeo, it's best to create a master in .mp4 format. This may change, of course, as technology continues to evolve, so it is important to check the specifications with the sites on which you'll be loading your video. In the future, watch HTML5 as it continues to evolve, because a standard video format may emerge that will change the game, although as I write there is yet to be agreement on which format to adopt.

Where to Post Your Video

So you've produced a phenomenal video that teaches viewers a key psychomotor skill or helps them understand an important topic. What now? You've got the video in your hot little hands but you need to make it available to your learners.

In the old days, you had a number of choices: you could run off some clunky old VHS tapes and send them to everyone who needed your lesson; you could buy some time on TV and have it scheduled; or you could arrange a showing in a training room and let everyone know to come and watch.

The good old days have been replaced by the good new days because you now have many more options. Of course, it depends upon your work. If you're a corporate trainer, the chances are you'll want it available on your internal corporate network. If you're a training contractor, you'll want to make it available to your clients outside. If you're running an educational site where people pay to watch your video, you'll need people to see it behind your paywall. If you're planning on publishing how-to videos and selling them, you can publish them as DVDs and sell those on the Internet.

So how do your viewers watch your video? And what are the implications and costs? Can you simply post it on your site? You have a number of choices about how to provide video content.

Download

If you choose to provide your video content as a download, you simply upload it to a website, ftp server, or file sharing site like Dropbox and let people click a button to download it. Naturally, the time it takes to download the video will depend on your video's file size and the speed of your viewer's Internet connection. Providing a file to download is different from providing it on a site like YouTube, because the complete video file will sit on the recipient's computer. With YouTube, the file sits on YouTube's server.

An advantage of downloading is that people have the complete video and can then watch it directly from their C drive without it pausing mid-play due to a slow Internet connection. They can also then take the video anywhere without needing an Internet connection. If you're a trainer delivering learning in, say, a factory where Internet connection is not easily accessible, this is a great option. However, the downside is that anyone can download your video file—you lose control over people being able to copy it.

Stream From Your Own Server

The second option is to stream your video. If you plan to stream your video—that is, enable people to watch it live, pause, and fast-forward it—you will need to post it to a media server that will allow people to stream it. You need to have a conversation with your IT department because there are a number of issues here that need to be addressed.

First, you'll need a media player on your website that will play the video. You can easily buy one. Second, you need to be sure that there is a lot of bandwidth between the media server and the Internet (or intranet if you're streaming within a company), because it may slow down if too many people access it at the same time. If you're a training contractor working for yourself, you may be tempted to set up your own media server at home in your basement, and this will require focus and patience.

The downside of a media server is that it requires real technical expertise beyond simply shooting and editing videos. Plus, it is expensive, because both the server and bandwidth cost a lot of money.

Post to a Video Sharing Site

The third option is to upload your video to a video sharing site like YouTube or Vimeo and then embed it in your website or learning program. The video sharing site acts as a media server to stream your video, plus it provides you with a media player. It will give you what's known as an embed code to insert on your website. Embedded content simply means that instead of displaying content from your website's server, the browser goes to another website for specific content, then automatically inserts it in your website. As far as the user is concerned, the content looks like it comes directly from your website when, in fact, it does not. What's good with video sharing sites is that not only do they place video on your site, but they also place a video player on your site.

More and more people are using sharing sites to situate video on their website, and there are significant benefits to it. The first benefit is that you don't need to run a media server. Running a media server is always tricky, especially when things go wrong. You really need to rely on your IT department to keep it operational and solve any problems. In my experience, most corporate IT departments are better skilled at running things like email exchanges and word processors rather than media applications. It can be frustrating waiting for them to learn the new skills in between their other responsibilities.

The second benefit is that you have streaming media for virtually no cost at all. YouTube doesn't charge you a penny, nor does Vimeo unless it is commercial content. If you want the upgraded subscription to provide your video in HD and take the Vimeo brand label off the media player embedded in your site, it will only cost $199 to upgrade to their commercial hosting service called Vimeo Pro. That's still incredibly cheap compared to hosting your own video.

Third, because the video is embedded on your site, but streamed from another site, you don't lose valuable bandwidth when people watch your videos. They are using the sharing site's bandwidth, not yours.

Fourth, you can generally upload your files in a number of different formats. Whether your master video is an .avi, .mp4, .wmv, or .mov file, these sites quickly convert it into .flv, which is universally available to anyone with an Internet browser. The folks who run these sites are whizzes when it comes to video technology—they take all the hassle from you and make sure it also plays on devices that don't allow Flash, like the iPad and iPhone.

One of the downsides of using sharing sites like YouTube is that you are sharing your video on the same platform as a teenage kid in Los Angeles who is video blogging from his bedroom. Having the YouTube logo on your professional video may not give you the status you want. For some it's fine, and for others, it's not.

Another downside with YouTube is that technically it's a social networking site. Many companies don't permit social networking sites through their firewalls, so you may have difficulties having viewers view your content. The same goes for Vimeo. Most people think of YouTube and Vimeo, but there are loads of other video sharing sites. These include Yahoo Video, Google Video, and Videojug Pages.

Host on a Commercial Video Platform

The fourth option is to host your video on a commercial video platform. Commercial companies offer an array of features that take the technical stress from your production schedule and enable your video to look professional. All you need to do is create great video and let them do the hard work. Most of the major newspapers and broadcasters around the world use commercial hosting platforms.

Most of these companies will enable you to customize the player and embed your logo on it. You can create channels so viewers search for content within the player or watch it much like they'd watch a TV schedule. These companies will provide tools to easily convert your video so it is mobile compatible on phones and tablets—and they provide sophisticated analytics along with robust systems that offer 99 percent up-time. You can find these providers by Googling "video platforms." Companies to look for include Brightcove, Viddler, Wistia, VBrick, and DaCast.

If you're a trainer working for yourself and don't fancy these commercial options, you may consider Vidmeup, which gives you many of the same options as the commercial sites, such as having video with your brand rather than YouTube's. Vidmeup is aimed at artists, although it does offer an affordable enterprise solution. At the time of printing, they also offer the option to build a paid video membership subscription, which is a great option for trainers, coaches, and speakers who have content they'd like to share with members.

Publish as DVDs

It may seem slightly yesterday, but believe it or not, many people still like to get their videos on DVDs. This demand will decrease. However, if you want to distribute your learning videos on discs, there are several options available to you.

First, there are many DVD fulfillment companies where you can upload your video file and then they will create DVD discs for you en masse. This saves you having to worry about duplicating them, which is time-consuming and cumbersome when you have other things to worry about.

Second, some companies will print individual discs on demand. It's similar to print on demand books. There are many companies offering these services around the U.S. and the best way to get a great price is to simply Google the phrase "DVD fulfillment" or "DVD on demand fulfillment."

Distributing Your Video

There are many ways to get your final video to people who need it. Simply choose the one that best serves your viewer. If it's DVD, work through a fulfillment house. If it's people who can access the web, you can stream it.

CHAPTER SIXTEEN

Video Workflow

In this chapter:

- Obstacles to efficient production
- Creating an optimum workflow

Be Disciplined

I remember that almost 20 years ago, when I was a radio talk show host, my boss Bruce McNeilly would wander into my studio at the end of a busy and grueling morning shift and say with a grin, "Beats work, huh?"

It was a neat joke, because while media production is hard, hard work, it can be exhilarating. Our team would roll into work at 5 a.m., be on air from 6 a.m. until 8:30 a.m., and then work through to 5 or 6 that night preparing for the following day's show. In fact, I'm told that psychologists equate the effort of a three-hour shift on air to a full eight-hour workday. But despite the hard work, we kept going back for more.

I share this not to reminisce but to point out that many people working in media are quickly hooked and the adrenaline and exhilaration can become an obsession. Soon we get so hooked on our new work that we forget some of the basic disciplines that ensure efficiency.

From years both working in and visiting radio and television stations and newspaper companies, I've discovered that success stories come not from people fueled by adrenaline, but from those who follow a disciplined approach to production. Unfortunately, the video production teams that I have seen in organizations that do not perform to a high standard lack this discipline and thus waste money and time. While I have seen this both in media companies and in nonmedia companies where I have consulted, it is more prevalent in corporate settings, where leaders do not know what efficient production looks like. Some of the corporate production I have seen would never be tolerated in a professional media environment.

A typical situation I see is where two or three staff are pooled together to create a video production unit. Often, they get their roles because they're either technically inclined and understand how video works on the Internet, or they have an interest in photography or amateur video. But their potential is not realized because they run into obstacles along the way to production that they have not been trained for.

Anyone can learn good production skills and develop a production discipline. So to help you do this, I want to spend the last few pages of the book highlighting some obstacles that often pop up and slow down production, as well as minimize the value of a production team to its organization. After we have gone through these, I will offer a step-by-step workflow that will optimize your personal and team efficiency. You can use the workflow as a checklist to measure your personal development as you learn to create didactic video.

Success Blockers

These are the top success blockers:

Lack of clarity of purpose. This results in a narrative that comes across as clumsy, the use of gratuitous special effects that don't add to the message, and endless revisions.

Creation of video for the sake of video. Whether it's a broadcaster, corporate communications unit, or learning department, some people are so hooked on video that they go looking for ways to use video and end up creating content no one watches because there was never any need for it. Or they find that video was not the best way to convey that information. Time and money are wasted on video creation, when a simple workbook or audio podcast may have been more effective.

Starting with words and not pictures. Rather than using pictures to pull the viewer through, they use words. This fails because people primarily watch video rather than listen to it.

Lack of a storyboard. This causes problems all the way through the production. When people don't think through the pictures first, the script tends to end up wordy and the pictures end up not as thorough. The camera operator ends up having to wing it for cutaways or guess camera positions on the fly, and generally does not have the time to scout out the most compelling shots. The editor wastes time trying to figure out the shots because they don't follow a nicely planned sequence. The editor also has to fix the shots because with a lack of planning, the shots often lack continuity.

Words trump the picture. Without a storyboard, words do the heavy lifting, and this results in heavy-handed video. Sometimes even with a storyboard, the writer does not write to picture, but repeats what's obvious and creates cognitive overload.

Breaks standard camera conventions. This is a very common cause of problems in the editing suite. People rely on auto functions and end up losing the opportunity to take crisp pictures and clear audio. When mistakes are made, some camera operators take the attitude, "Oh well, I guess we can fix it in the edit." Sure, but it triples production time.

Become obsessed with special effects. Video editing software packages are amazing and offer all sorts of fun effects. Most of them are irrelevant to the average didactic video. However, some novices get so excited about starbursts and blind dissolves that they litter them throughout the video. Instead of noticing the message, we notice the editing.

Over-reliance on special effects. Some novices get excited by clever tricks such as chroma-key. They then over-rely on shooting with green screen rather than going out and getting shots in the field. Chroma-key is great, but it takes extra time to render.

Creating a Workflow for Learning Video

Taking some of these issues into consideration, here is a workflow that I follow when creating didactic video.

1. Start With a Learning Objective

Before you start doodling a storyboard on the back of a napkin, clarify your learning objective. What will the learner learn from your video? Most learning professionals have been taught

Mager's principles of writing learning objectives. Follow Mager's principles and start the video production process with an objective just as you would if you were planning a training session. The more explicit your learning objective is, the easier it will be to evaluate every element of your video, to ensure that it works at achieving the objective.

Another point to consider: Don't cram your video with loads of objectives. Set one objective and keep your video as short as it needs to be to achieve that objective. It's more effective to spend five minutes reinforcing the same point so viewers remember it than cramming in five objectives that they will forget.

2. Define Your Audience

Who is your learner? Teaching CPR to a medical professional will be different from teaching it to a member of the public. What is your viewer's level of expertise? This will help you work out what analogies to use and what assumptions you can make about their prior knowledge and expertise. Under what conditions are they learning? A medical professional may be watching the video in a break room, whereas a member of the public may be watching at home.

3. Ask If Video Is the Best Method

When you are clear about your learning objective and who the learner is, ask yourself if video is the best tool to facilitate learning. Remember, video must be visual and it can't handle complex or abstract theories. CPR works because it is visual. Legal policy or accounting rules probably will not work well in video. Be ruthless, because video takes time and money to create. If video is not the best option, save yourself the bother and save your viewer the time.

4. Do Your Research

Now that you have determined that video will indeed create an effective learning experience, it's time to do the research. We're talking here about classic instructional design work. Do a work and task analysis and get to know your topic inside out. Read up on it and interview some subject matter experts. Make sure you are up to speed on the latest techniques.

5. Brainstorm Story Ideas

Sit down and start thinking through how you may convey the learning objective visually. What stories can you use? What existing mental structures will your viewer have that you can tap into? What's the best way to convey the information? Role plays, demonstrations, interviews, graphics?

For a video on CPR, you might choose a demo, a series of text graphics to reinforce your objective, and an interview or two: perhaps with a survivor about their CPR experience, or with an expert who performs CPR regularly.

If you plan a demo or role play, go and visit the location where you will film it to think about camera position and angles. It's a good idea not to act solo at this stage—talk to colleagues or get them involved in the brainstorming. Keep notes of your thoughts and conversations. Start thinking about any music you plan to use, and what it would achieve narratively.

6. Draw a Storyboard

Now that you have a general idea about your video, it's time to create a storyboard. Remember, a storyboard is not art, but is a visual sketch of what the viewer should see. It forces you to think about where you will place the camera (which saves time when shooting on location), what shot size to use, what camera angle, and what to have in shot or out of shot. You may find yourself doing several drafts and playing around with it until you are happy. When you are close to finishing, share it with your subject matter expert to be sure you're on track. If someone else will be editing the video, get their comments. They'll have ideas you may not have considered, and it will get their minds ready for your project. When you review your storyboard, ask yourself how each shot helps achieve your learning objective. If there is any shot or effect in the storyboard that you can't show achieves the learning objective, take it out.

7. Write the Script

You have the storyboard; now it's time to write the script. Remember, the picture tells the story so any commentary, dialogue, or monologue must add new information to the picture. Follow the conventions we discussed in chapter 7. When you have this, you should have a two-columned script that you can circulate to people involved in the production. Make sure your subject matter expert signs off.

8. Plan Your Shoot

You've got your script and location primed—now it's time to plan your shoot. This means: checking with facility management offices for permission to film; making sure you have parking permits if it involves driving to a location; booking equipment; lining up actors for demos and role plays; and lining up experts for interviews. It means buying or checking that you have licenses for any music you plan to use, and conducting a risk assessment so you're ready for anything that may go wrong. You might also start work on any graphics you need to insert into the video.

9. Shoot Your Video

Now you're ready: Head out and shoot the video. Follow your script and keep your storyboard handy for any last-minute reminders about how a shot should look. When you're on location, look out for any visual element that is not in your storyboard that you can shoot and take back to edit as a backup cutaway. It's a good idea to have the subject matter expert with you to sign off that each shot is accurate.

10. Ingest and Log Your Footage

After the shoot, come back to the office and ingest your video footage. Give each shot a filename that follows your standard convention. Write any notes you need for each individual shot and add any metadata such as "CU of CPR sign," in case the footage can be used for other projects. Check that each clip's quality is good enough. If not, perform the correction now and save it so it's ready for editing. Disciplined operators will ingest and take care of these disciplines as soon as they return the camera. Even if they're not going to edit the footage right away, good operators won't leave it to the last minute and ingest the footage just before they start editing.

11. Conduct the Edit

When you're ready, it's time to edit everything together. That means positioning your video and graphics along the storyboard or timeline in your editing software, trimming each shot, adding effects, and then exporting. You may find that you need to go back and reshoot some footage. If you have planned well, this will not be necessary. When you have edited the video, create a low-resolution copy to circulate to whoever signs off on the video and also to the subject matter expert. Make sure the subject matter expert gives her approval. When you're ready, export the master copy.

12. Have a Glass of Champagne

I know we're talking about web video and not television. But a few years back, there was a time-honored tradition of celebrating the success of a television production with a glass of wine and some snacks. Celebrate your success! After all, it beats work.

Index

A

B

E

F

G

H

I

J

K

L

T

V

W

Y

Z

About the Author

Jonathan Halls has been teaching media and learning for more than 20 years. He started teaching digital and new media as part of the BBC's New Media Training Unit in 1999, focusing on editorial content. Today he runs a specialist training firm in Washington, D.C., which specializes in media, communication, and leadership training. He is an adjunct professor at George Washington University.

Formerly based in the United Kingdom, Jonathan used to run the BBC's highly respected production training department, where he was responsible for the delivery of training in all aspects of television production, radio operations, and new media. During his time there, he delivered training while some of the biggest changes affecting broadcasting for a generation took place. Prior to his role as learning executive, he was the skills training manager in the BBC new media training unit, where he expanded the unit's offerings in editorial training as well as enhanced its pedagogical processes.

After the BBC, he was managing director of Talk Show Communication Ltd. in London, which delivered training throughout Europe in digital media production and leadership. At this time, Jonathan delivered multimedia training to newspaper companies that were making the transition from paper and ink to digital publishing. He did this in the U.K., France, Germany, Netherlands, Portugal, Russia, India, and Egypt through his partnership with Ifra Newsplex. Many of these were large scale change projects that included the much reported Daily Telegraph change project in London.

Today, Jonathan runs his own training practice in the Washington D.C. area: Jonathan Halls & Associates. He divides his time between running workshops for nonmedia professionals in the skills of media production with low cost equipment, and delivering leadership and change workshops for corporate clients. He also runs a limited number of workshops and master classes for media companies. His special focus is on leadership communication and innovation. Jonathan is also interested in the transition we are experiencing as we change from an industrial to post-industrial society, with its implications for organizational effectiveness and professional resilience.

Jonathan has worked as a trainer, communications manager, media executive, journalist, and talk show host. He has a bachelor's and a master's degree in adult education from the University of Technology, Sydney. He is an active member of the American Society for Training and Development, where he has served on the planning advisory committees for its international conference (reviewing leadership proposals) and its TechKnowledge conference. He was on the review panel for ASTD's BEST Awards for Learning Organizations, and was founding president of ASTD's U.K. Global Network in 2003. He is a member of ASTD's metro D.C. chapter, as well as a member of the National Speakers' Association metro D.C. chapter.